Crimes Against Children:
Child Abuse and Neglect

CRIME, JUSTICE, AND PUNISHMENT

Crimes Against Children:
Child Abuse and Neglect

Tracee de Hahn

Austin Sarat, GENERAL EDITOR

CHELSEA HOUSE PUBLISHERS
Philadelphia

Chelsea House Publishers

Editor in Chief Stephen Reginald
Managing Editor James D. Gallagher
Production Manager Pamela Loos
Art Director Sara Davis
Director of Photography Judy L. Hasday
Senior Production Editor LeeAnne Gelletly

Staff for CRIMES AGAINST CHILDREN

Senior Editor John Ziff
Associate Art Director Takeshi Takahashi
Designer Keith Trego
Picture Researcher Patricia Burns
Cover Illustrator Janet Hamlin

First Printing

1 3 5 7 9 8 6 4 2

The Chelsea House World Wide Web address is
http://www.chelseahouse.com

Library of Congress Cataloging-in-Publication Data

De Hahn, Tracee.
Crimes against children: child abuse and neglect /
Tracee de Hahn; Austin Sarat, general editor.
    p. cm. — (Crime, justice, and punishment)
Includes bibliographical references and index.

ISBN 0-7910-4253-7 (hardcover)

1. Child abuse—United States. 2. Children—Crimes
against—United States. 3. Child welfare—United States.
I. Sarat, Austin. II. Title. III. Series.
HV6626.52.D4 2000
362.76'0973—dc21   99-43549
                                                  CIP

Contents

CRIME, JUSTICE, AND PUNISHMENT

Fears and Fascinations:

An Introduction to
Crime, Justice, and Punishment

By Austin Sarat

e live with crime and images of crime all around us. Crime evokes in most of us a deep aversion, a feeling of profound vulnerability, but it also evokes an equally deep fascination. Today, in major American cities the fear of crime is a major fact of life, some would say a disproportionate response to the realities of crime. Yet the fear of crime is real, palpable in the quickened steps and furtive glances of people walking down darkened streets. At the same time, we eagerly follow crime stories on television and in movies. We watch with a "who done it" curiosity, eager to see the illicit deed done, the investigation undertaken, the miscreant brought to justice and given his just deserts. On the streets the presence of crime is a reminder of our own vulnerability and the precariousness of our taken-for-granted rights and freedoms. On television and in the movies the crime story gives us a chance to probe our own darker motives, to ask "Is there a criminal within?" as well as to feel the collective satisfaction of seeing justice done.

Fear and fascination, these two poles of our engagement with crime, are, of course, only part of the story. Crime is, after all, a major social and legal problem, not just an issue of our individual psychology. Politicians today use our fear of, and fascination with, crime for political advantage. How we respond to crime, as well as to the political uses of the crime issue, tells us a lot about who we are as a people as well as what we value and what we tolerate. Is our response compassionate or severe? Do we seek to understand or to punish, to enact an angry vengeance or to rehabilitate and welcome the criminal back into our midst? The CRIME, JUSTICE, AND PUNISHMENT series is designed to explore these themes, to ask why we are fearful and fascinated, to probe the meanings and motivations of crimes and criminals and of our responses to them, and, finally, to ask what we can learn about ourselves and the society in which we live by examining our responses to crime.

Crime is always a challenge to the prevailing normative order and a test of the values and commitments of law-abiding people. It is sometimes a Raskolnikov-like act of defiance, an assertion of the unwillingness of some to live according to the rules of conduct laid out by organized society. In this sense, crime marks the limits of the law and reminds us of law's all-too-regular failures. Yet sometimes there is more desperation than defiance in criminal acts; sometimes they signal a deep pathology or need in the criminal. To confront crime is thus also to come face-to-face with the reality of social difference, of class privilege and extreme deprivation, of race and racism, of children neglected, abandoned, or abused whose response is to enact on others what they have experienced themselves. And occasionally crime, or what is labeled a criminal act, represents a call for justice, an appeal to a higher moral order against the inadequacies of existing law.

Figuring out the meaning of crime and the motivations of criminals and whether crime arises from defiance, desperation, or the appeal for justice is never an easy task. The motivations and meanings of crime are as varied as are the persons who engage in criminal conduct. They are as mysterious as any of the mysteries of the human soul. Yet the desire to know the secrets of crime and the criminal is a strong one, for in that knowledge may lie one step on the road to protection, if not an assurance of one's own personal safety. Nonetheless, as strong as that desire may be, there is no available technology that can allow us to know the whys of crime with much confidence, let alone a scientific certainty. We can, however, capture something about crime by studying the defiance, desperation, and quest for justice that may be associated with it. Books in the CRIME, JUSTICE, AND PUNISHMENT series will take up that challenge. They tell stories of crime and criminals, some famous, most not, some glamorous and exciting, most mundane and commonplace.

This series will, in addition, take a sober look at American criminal justice, at the procedures through which we investigate crimes and identify criminals, at the institutions in which innocence or guilt is determined. In these procedures and institutions we confront the thrill of the chase as well as the challenge of protecting the rights of those who defy our laws. It is through the efficiency and dedication of law enforcement that we might capture the criminal; it is in the rare instances of their corruption or brutality that we feel perhaps our deepest betrayal. Police, prosecutors, defense lawyers, judges, and jurors administer criminal justice and in their daily actions give substance to the guarantees of the Bill of Rights. What is an adversarial system of justice? How does it work? Why do we have it? Books in the CRIME, JUSTICE, AND PUNISHMENT series will examine the thrill of the chase as we seek to capture the criminal. They will also reveal the drama and majesty of the criminal trial as well as the day-to-day reality of a criminal justice system in which trials are the exception and negotiated pleas of guilty are the rule.

When the trial is over or the plea has been entered, when we have separated the innocent from the guilty, the moment of punishment has arrived. The injunction to punish the guilty, to respond to pain inflicted by inflicting pain, is as old as civilization itself. "An eye for an eye and a tooth for a tooth" is a biblical reminder that punishment must measure pain for pain. But our response to the criminal must be better than and different from the crime itself. The biblical admonition, along with the constitutional prohibition of "cruel and unusual punishment," signals that we seek to punish justly and to be just not only in the determination of who can and should be punished, but in how we punish as well. But neither reminder tells us what to do with the wrongdoer. Do we rape the rapist, or burn the home of the arsonist? Surely justice and decency say no. But, if not, then how can and should we punish? In a world in which punishment is neither identical to the crime nor an automatic response to it, choices must be made and we must make them. Books in the CRIME, JUSTICE, AND PUNISHMENT series will examine those choices and the practices, and politics, of punishment. How do we punish and why do we punish as we do? What can we learn about the rationality and appropriateness of today's responses to crime by examining our past and its responses? What works? Is there, and can there be, a just measure of pain?

CRIME, JUSTICE, AND PUNISHMENT brings together books on some of the great themes of human social life. The books in this series capture our fear and fascination with crime and examine our responses to it. They remind us of the deadly seriousness of these subjects. They bring together themes in law, literature, and popular culture to challenge us to think again, to think anew, about subjects that go to the heart of who we are and how we can and will live together.

* * * * *

Given the special status of children in our culture, crimes against children seem particularly heinous. And what is generally true is even more compelling when the perpetrators of crimes against children are their parents or other caregivers. Because of the almost automatic revulsion that these crimes generate, they also challenge our justice system. The challenge that they pose is in fact twofold. First, can law devise effective protections for children and punishment that deters those who might otherwise victimize them? Second, can law ensure that those accused of crimes against children receive fair treatment?

Because crimes against children are so often perpetrated by their caregivers, these crimes challenge conventional ideas of family and family life. They require us to rethink ideas of privacy. At the same time, the effort to prevent or detect these crimes may invite forms of state intervention that threaten important public values. And efforts like Megan's Law, which provides for notification when someone who has been convicted and punished for perpetrating acts of violence against children moves into a community, raise serious issues of fairness. How do we balance the rights of people to be protected from crime against the rights of people who have paid their debts to society?

Crimes Against Children speaks to these questions as it provides an in-depth examination of child abuse and neglect. Who are the perpetrators of these crimes? What effects do they have on their victims? How can and should society respond? Combining careful historical analysis and compelling stories of individual cases, this book advances our understanding of some of the most serious issues facing the legal system today.

WILL YOU BE MY MOMMY?

Six-year-old Elisa Izquierdo cried, "Mommy, please stop! I'm sorry." These were familiar sounds to neighbors living adjacent to apartment 20A in the Rutgers House housing project in Lower Manhattan. Although some neighbors cringed and turned up their television sets, no one called police. Then, on the afternoon of November 20, 1995, the cries stopped. Two days later Elisa's mother, Awilda Inpez, had a chilling conversation with her own sister. Awilda said that Elisa "was on the bed like retarded. Not eating or drinking or going to the bathroom." Elisa's aunt offered to take care of the other children so Elisa could be taken to the hospital, but Awilda responded that she would think about it "after she did the dishes." By the time Awilda allowed a neighbor to call police, her six-year-old daughter was dead.

Children are society's most vulnerable members. More than 2 million American kids may suffer abuse and neglect every year.

13

Elisa had lived with her mother and five half-siblings in apartment 20A for a little over a year. During that time she had deteriorated from the little girl teachers described as "radiant" with a "brilliant smile" to a battered statistic. When firefighter Michael Brown arrived at the apartment two days before Thanksgiving and began performing cardiopulmonary resuscitation (CPR) on Elisa's motionless body, he knew that it was hopeless. Elisa was covered with bruises and cuts, bones in her hand were protruding through her skin, and her head had been partially crushed.

Elisa's story should not have ended so tragically. Because of her mother's history of drug abuse, sole custody of Elisa Izquierdo had initially been assigned to her doting father when her parents broke up. Unfortunately, that did not last long. Elisa's mother went through a drug-treatment program, married, then in November 1991 won the right to have Elisa visit every other weekend. Elisa's father and teachers immediately noticed a change in the little girl. Upon returning to her father's house she would throw up and refuse to enter the bathroom. When teachers reported the behavior to city social workers, they allowed the visits to continue after Awilda promised not to hit or spank Elisa.

Then the unimaginable happened: Elisa's father died suddenly of cancer, and the court sent her to live full-time with her mother. A year and a half later, Elisa was dead. In retrospect, the court's decision to give the little girl back to her mother may seem ill-advised, even reckless, but it was by no means unique. Laws in the United States favor keeping biological families together. And despite fierce opposition from Elisa's father's relatives and from teachers, this was the outcome social workers advocated.

Why was Elisa living in an abusive household when relatives and teachers were suspicious? Caseworkers in New York claim that the system failed, overburdened by the sheer number of abuse charges that must be

investigated. Child advocates blame current laws that, they claim, keep too many children in abusive homes based on a parent's promise to correct behavior.

According to current statistics, more than 1.1 million documented cases of child abuse occur each year in the United States. However, many experts suspect that the true number is at least twice that.

Like most crimes, child abuse requires that the offender have a specific intent to commit a criminal deed and that he or she act on that intent. Given the dependence of children on adult caregivers, however, much harm can be done even without criminal intent. The failure to provide for a child's basic needs—an act of omission rather than one of commission—is called neglect.

Endangered children, a term popularized in the 1980s, encompasses children who suffer physical or sexual abuse as well as those who are neglected. Each state creates its own definitions of these three condi-

Six-year-old Elisa Izquierdo lies in her coffin. The young girl was beaten to death by her mother.

tions, but common themes can be found.

Physical abuse is typically defined as nonaccidental physical injury. While the extreme beatings Elisa Izquierdo suffered clearly fall under this definition, other, equally fatal, forms of physical abuse are harder to detect. Violently shaking a baby, for example, can cause brain damage and death, but it leaves no external injuries. Because of this, the deaths of many infants and small children caused by what doctors have labeled "shaken baby syndrome" may go undetected as physical abuse. Most physical abuse of children, as in the case of Elisa Izquierdo, occurs within the family.

Sexual abuse is typically defined as any sexual activity between an adult and a child, or the sexual exploitation of a child for the gratification or profit of an adult. Inherent in the definition is the belief that a child—termed a minor in a court of law—cannot be responsible for making certain decisions. This means that even if a child were to consent to have sex with an adult, the adult would still be guilty of sexual abuse. Within the broad definition of sexual abuse, there exists a range of acts, from the physical trauma of forced penetration and inappropriate fondling to the psychological trauma of immoral suggestions or "flash-ing" (exposing oneself). Regardless of the degree of physical involvement, all of these situations constitute sexual abuse because they invade a child's physical and emotional security.

There is a common misperception that predatory strangers constitute the greatest threat of sexually abus-ing children. The fact is that most sexually abused chil-dren are victimized by family members and friends. Specifically, about 30 percent are abused by a relative and 60 percent by a trusted friend or neighbor. By contrast, only 10 percent of sexually abused children are victimized by a stranger. When strangers do sexually abuse a child, physical force is usually involved. Abuse within the circle of family and friends, on the other hand, typically involves subtle threats or psychological coercion. "If you ever tell anyone, I'll go to jail, the family will be broken up, and you will be taken from your mom and me forever," an abusive father or stepfather might say. Other concerns may influence older children. They might submit to sexual abuse to spare a younger sister or brother from harm, or they might be embarrassed by the thought of friends and neighbors learning what has happened. Many times they are ashamed, mistakenly believing they brought the abuse upon themselves.

The third and broadest form of abuse, neglect, is more difficult to define than are physical and sexual abuse. Neglect generally includes failure by a parent or caregiver to provide minimally adequate food, clothing, shelter, education, or medical care. A great deal of media attention focuses on crimes of brutality like the killing of Elisa Izquierdo, but physical abuse represents only 25 percent of the total number of documented abuse cases in the United States. Neglect is far more common. While the results of neglect might not be as overtly dramatic as are those of physical or sexual abuse, they can be just as devastating for the approximately 500,000 children affected every year. Sustained neglect can have significant and far-reaching effects on a child's development and future abilities.

Hoping to provide guidance on standards of care, the Utah Supreme Court remarked in 1987, "Children are entitled to the care of an adult who cares enough to provide the child with the opportunity to form psychological bonds, in addition to the physical necessities of life. . . . An unfit or incompetent parent is one who substantially and repeatedly refuses or fails to render proper parental care and protection."

However, judges remain hesitant to intervene in families when poverty is the reason a child's needs are not met. As the Massachusetts Supreme Court wrote in 1985, "A parent may not be found unfit because he or

Violently shaking a baby can cause brain damage and even death, but it leaves no external injuries. Experts believe that this kind of abuse often goes undetected.

she is poor." Determining whether a child's problems are caused by poverty or maltreatment is often a difficult task. Complicating that, neglect is reported most often among single parents who are under economic stress and who are in charge of a large number of children. This places continual pressure on social workers, teachers, and physicians to correctly determine when the line has been crossed and a child is being neglected. These professionals have to make a decision based on thoughtful consideration of the evidence without allowing themselves to be pressured by an atmosphere of hysteria; simultaneously they must not overlook the real possibility that the safety of a child may hang in the balance.

Before authorities can intervene to protect children from abuse of any variety, a credible suspicion that abuse is occurring must be brought to their attention. This may occur when the victimized child tells a parent, teacher, or pediatrician or when an adult notices signs of abuse and notifies authorities. Often the next step is to prevent contact between the abuser and the child. For Elisa Izquierdo this could have meant removal to a foster home. Sometimes the abuser is arrested and jailed. However, for a police officer to make an arrest, he or she must have probable cause. This is a vague legal concept that means that the officer must possess trustworthy information that would lead a reasonable person to believe that a crime was committed by a particular person.

Cases of neglect can prove even harder to sort out. For example, determining whether neglect was involved in near-drowning incidents, a large number of which occur every year in bathtubs, is frequently tricky.

One such case involved two sisters. Two-year-old Jamie splashed her four-year-old sister, Erica, with soapy water despite her sister's unwillingness to play. The two girls were taking their baths together, something the younger Jamie loved. Tonight their mother left the two girls alone for a few minutes, with the older Erica "in charge."

Jamie listened as her mother continued to talk to the girls from the next room. Curious, she placed her face in the tub water to see if she could still hear. Satisfied that she could, even though the words were dim and hollow, Jamie tried to raise her head to take a breath. But she couldn't move. Her long hair was trapped under her sister's legs. When she slapped the water to get her sister's attention, Erica, tired of her baby sister's antics, didn't turn to look. When Jamie opened her mouth to call for help she swallowed water.

A short time later, when their mother looked in on the bathing girls, she found Jamie's head underwater. Jamie was lucky; her mother knew CPR. Even before the ambulance arrived Jamie was breathing on her own.

Many children are not as fortunate as Jamie. Neglect that leads to drowning is one of the leading causes of death in children under five years of age. In a study of urban emergency-room cases of near-drowning, 21 of 88 patients had been in a bathtub. The majority of patients were under two years of age, and 80 percent of the children had been alone for less than five minutes. In nearly one-third of the cases the children were in the bathtub with other children, although all of the children were under four years of age.

Because of the scope of the problem, physicians are being asked to evaluate cases of near-drowning in bathtubs for signs of possible child abuse or neglect. But this is more difficult than it sounds. It involves a judgment call on the part of the physician: was the few minutes Jamie's mother left the girls alone neglect or simply the prelude to an unfortunate accident? Further complicating this, in many cases the physician has to rely solely on the parent's version of what happened. Without concrete evidence (a history of accidents or other injuries), the physician sometimes lacks the probable cause necessary to make an accusation. Because of this, it remains difficult to determine whether the incident was an isolated accident or part of a larger pattern of neglect.

Other forms of neglect are easier to identify, but first they need to be discovered. One such horror story was uncovered in February 1994 when police in Chicago found 19 children jammed into a cold and squalid apartment on Keystone Avenue. Horrified officers saw roaches scooting past rat droppings and bowls of rotting spaghetti next to a flour sack crawling with bugs. One child pleaded with officers, "Will you be my mommy?" Two toddlers were sharing a bone with a terrier mutt. Added to this was evidence of physical abuse. One boy, already crippled by cerebral palsy, had been burned and whipped. Sitting amidst the chaos and horror were six women—the mothers of the 19 children. Between them the women were collecting $4,692 a month in welfare and food stamps for the "care of their children." Chicago police officers seized the kids and turned them over to Cook County's Juvenile Court.

The Keystone kids, as they came to be called, were placed in the court of Judge Lynne Kawamoto. Here their story took a very different turn from that of Elisa Izquierdo. Despite having served in the Abuse and Neglect Division of the Cook County Court system for only one month, Judge Kawamoto did not hesitate to act in a way contrary to the long-standing goal of keeping children with their biological families. While she did not look forward to choosing between the sanctity of families and the security of the children, she also was unwilling to accept the promise of the mothers that they would no longer neglect their children. At the same time, Judge Kawamoto realized that, aside from

the death penalty, there is no ruling more final in the American judicial system than the termination of parental rights.

After three years of rulings, Judge Kawamoto ensured that none of the Keystone kids would ever return to his or her natural parents; all but those already old enough to live on their own would be adopted. In the end the judge may have prevented the Keystone kids from becoming another statistic like Elisa Izquierdo and the 1,000 to 2,000 children who die every year in America as a result of abuse and neglect. Warning signs were present with many of those victims, but evaluating the actual risk to endangered children is a difficult task rife with uncertainties. Plus, other factors enter the equation: the rights of parents, the goal of giving the child stability, and, perhaps most important, the idea that the family—even if it may be somewhat dysfunctional—is sacrosanct.

Numerous cases of near-drowning occur every year among toddlers in bathtubs. Determining whether such incidents result from neglect—and therefore whether action must be taken to protect the child's welfare—can be extremely difficult.

THE LONG ROAD TO FAMILY

The sanctity of the family—which judges, social workers, police, and physicians have to confront every time an accusation of abuse within the family arises—is a 20th-century idea. Throughout most of the century, the family's "natural" structure (male breadwinner, female homemaker) was viewed as self-evident, and child-rearing was seen as its central task.

Historically, however, the family was a much more fluid institution, and children were not at its center. In fact, for many hundreds of years the high infant-mortality rate, combined with constant economic pressure, created a world where children were often treated as little more than commodities. This was true

An immigrant family in its one-room tenement, early 1900s. In the view of the middle and upper classes, the communal lifestyle of the poor was inherently detrimental to child development, and poor parents were almost by definition considered unfit.

Mary, Queen of Scots at age 16. More than 10 years earlier her relatives had sent her to France to be raised by strangers and, eventually, married to the heir to the French throne. By contemporary Western standards, such treatment would be considered neglect, even abandonment.

at both ends of the economic spectrum.

In 1548, five-year-old Mary stood on the deck of a ship and stared across the gray sea at the coastline of Scotland. It was a sight she never expected to see again. Queen of Scotland since she was one week old, Mary may have been envied by the young girls standing on shore watching the ship sail away. Certainly her fine velvet cloak and jeweled rings would have been admired. However, the reality was far different from the appearance of a life of ease, wealth, and power.

Since birth young Mary had been a pawn in her adult relatives' game of international strategy. The young Queen Mary had certainly heard at least one uncle say, What good are royal princesses unless they can be married to secure armies for their native land? Because of this Mary, Queen of Scots sailed from her home before her sixth birthday to live among strangers at the French court, where she would be raised by her future husband's family. A great adventure for a five-year-old girl, yes. But it was also a life of loneliness and responsibility all too common for princesses for hundreds of years.

Was this neglect, even abandonment? In the modern Western world the answer would be yes. In a 1944 decision known as *Price v. Massachusetts*, the United States Supreme Court declared, "It is in the interest of youth itself, that children be both safeguarded from abuses and given the opportunities for growth into free and independent citizens."

Betrothed at five and sent to live among strangers, Mary was clearly not allowed to grow into a free and independent citizen, despite her status as queen. But these are 20th-century ideas, and before passing judgment on the treatment of a 16th-century girl, one must look at the evolution of children in the family.

From the dawn of the Middle Ages, the position of children has gradually changed, culminating in the creation of the modern family unit, in which children are seen as the central element of a nurturing environment. In medieval times, however, the happiness of children was secondary to the larger concern of survival. The family was not a sentimental unit, but an economic and social one.

A large factor in the treatment—or to modern sensibility, neglect—of medieval children was the high mortality rate among the very young. The high rate of deaths, caused by poor nutrition and lack of medical knowledge, helped create a different idea of family relationships than we know today. Too many children died for their parents to become emotionally attached to a newborn baby.

Even the educated elite supported this attitude. Michel de Montaigne (1533–92), the French essayist and moralist, observed, "I have lost two or three children in their infancy, not without regret, but without great sorrow." Most people probably agreed with Montaigne when he stated, "Children have neither mental activities nor recognizable bodily shape." Montaigne also wrote about the ingenious antics of infancy as interesting to adults "for our amusement, like monkeys." This indicates the tip of a large iceberg of apathy regarding the welfare and development of children. One can only imagine the status of poor children in a society in which wealthy intellectuals were uninterested. From birth until an age when they could perform tasks important to the economic survival of the family, children existed on the periphery of the social unit of the family. This was apparent at both ends of the social spectrum, from princess to pauper.

Although Mary, Queen of Scots would have been adequately fed, clothed, and even instructed in the skills necessary for her life at the French court, she would not have received the kind of nurturing that modern science recommends for the development of a happy, healthy child. Her Scottish and French relatives spent the first five years of Mary's life planning how

A man assaults his family. Throughout most of history, a father's treatment of his family, and particularly his children, wasn't seen as a legitimate concern of the state.

best to capitalize on her royal title by sending her to a more advantageous (to them) position in France. Mary knew from a very early age that she would leave the familiarity of her home. Thus for her and her relatives, any sentimental attachment was both harmful and frivolous. At the other end of the social spectrum, children were a drain on the food resources of the family until they were old enough to share in the family labor.

All children were considered miniature replicas of their parents, either as tiny courtiers or as tired workers. Even in play children did not have games or toys separate from those of adults until the 15th century, and then the toys were miniature versions of items used by adults in everyday life, such as the wooden hobbyhorse (a representation of a horse, then the main form of transportation).

However, this apparent lack of concern for the well-being of children does not mean that they were not important to family life. They simply had to reach the age of productivity, whether through profitable marriage or ability to work. Then they were a family's most important asset. Up until the 20th century, large families meant more physical help for parents struggling to survive.

If we apply modern attitudes, it appears that most children in the past were neglected. Young girls were expected to share the duties of their mother in everything from cooking and cleaning to rearing the younger children, some only a year or two younger than the tiny caregiver. Boys shouldered farm labor, provided food, or apprenticed to learn a trade with the understanding that every mouth needed to earn its own keep. But did self-sufficiency and hard work mean children were not loved? Not necessarily. Their lifestyle was economic necessity. This same question concerning neglect is still asked today. Wealthy parents may hire a baby-sitter to be in the house so they can work outside in the garden or run an errand. Poorer parents may leave their children alone in the house to do similar tasks. Until an accident occurs that causes harm to the unsupervised child, the poorer parent might not be called neglectful.

The end of the 17th century brought a change that would eventually have a profound impact on family life and that even today complicates the issue of child abuse. Until this time privacy had been almost non-existent throughout society. Most families slept in one room. Even in wealthy households the idea of a room primarily for sleep did not exist, and when night fell, folding beds were set up in the most convenient corner. In wealthy households of the late 17th century, however, the use of permanent bedrooms came into vogue. This was only one manifestation of the new idea of privacy. Servants who formerly had slept in the rooms of their masters, and had therefore shared every intimate moment with them, were banished to other parts of the house, thereby excluding them from certain aspects of the family's private life.

Understandably, change occurred at a much slower pace among the poor, who lacked the economic resources to create separate sleeping rooms. Up until the 20th century the poor in many cases lived crowded together in one or two rooms and continued to share not only sleeping rooms but also beds. But by the beginning of the 18th century the steadily extending zone of private life had begun to exclude outsiders from the affairs of even poor families.

If outsiders no longer *saw* the inner workings of the family, they had never had any *say* in the treatment of children. As head of the household, the father had, from ancient times, been given the power to treat his children as he saw fit. Children were commodities; they had never been recognized as having rights independent of their parents.

By the 18th century, children still had no defined rights, but fundamental changes occurred in the way kids were viewed. Ideas put forth by thinkers such as the English philosopher John Locke (1632–1704) and the French philosopher Jean-Jacques Rousseau (1712–78) brought health and education to the forefront of parents' minds. The ideas of Locke and Rousseau were part of a greater movement, termed the Enlightenment, that swept across Europe and into the young colonies of America.

Before Locke published his "Essay Concerning Human Understanding" in 1690, the predominant belief was that children were miniature adults of predetermined abilities and disposition, products of their inherited traits. Locke, however, suggested that at birth a baby's mind was a "tabula rasa," or blank slate. The child's "sense-impressions," or experiences, would be "written" upon that slate, thus determining the kind of adult he or she would become. Providing the right environment for a child's growth and development was therefore essential, and Locke recommended a rigorous physical, mental, and moral education. He also believed that parents, as the most powerful examples for their children, should take an active role in this education.

Jean-Jacques Rousseau, born a few years after Locke's death, experienced the Enlightenment at its height. Like Locke, Rousseau believed that a child's environment and experiences were important to his or her development. But he also believed that the child should develop at his or her own pace. The idea of every child engaging in exploration to suit his or her needs and interests was a giant step from Locke's belief in the carefully structured environment of child development.

While the theories were different, the result was the same: focus was shifted to the child as an important part of the family, whom parents should guide toward adulthood. Of course, change came gradually, and Enlightenment ideas about child-rearing didn't spread evenly across all socioeconomic groups.

In fact, as the 19th century unfolded, a great divide opened between the children of prosperous parents and the children of poor parents. Poor children typically received little education, lived in a single room with their families, and worked long hours from an early age. Upper-class children experienced dramatically different childhoods. Educated and well-off parents of the 19th century were themselves products of the Enlightenment and continued to place importance on the surroundings and development of their children. Wealthy parents hired tutors and nurses, creating a careful atmosphere for their children's development and learning. Childhood was viewed as an idyllic time, a time of innocence, and the young were excluded from both knowledge of

A little scrubber girl from the West 52nd Street Industrial School in New York City, circa 1890. Nineteenth-century reformers attempted to save poor children from a life of physical and moral squalor by sending them to so-called work schools to learn job skills and middle-class values. Many of these arrangements amounted to little more than the economic exploitation of the children.

and participation in the adult world. Not only did children of the upper classes no longer sleep in their parents' bedroom but they also did not eat with them or actively engage in play together. Contact between wealthy parents and their children was limited to periodic visits to the nursery, which was the domain of nurse and tutor.

The ideal of the private, sanctified domestic family, invented in England during the Victorian era (1819–1901) to shore up a created image of the family, romanticized middle-class families and abhorred the more communal lifestyle of the poor. It also conveniently ignored a disturbing reality: much of the wealth that Victorian England amassed and that the upper classes enjoyed came at the expense of the poor, who toiled long hours for subsistence wages. While upper-class Victorians decried the physical and moral squalor in which poor children grew up, by the mid-1800s many of these children were working in mines and factories, 14 to 16 hours a day, seven days a week, for a pittance. The popular novelist Charles Dickens was among those who pointed out these contradictions. Himself a child of poverty in Victorian England, Dickens harshly criticized the cruelty that children suffered at the hands of a society that claimed to be concerned about their welfare.

The plight of children was also a concern for 19th-century reformers in the United States. Like their English counterparts, these reformers were influenced by John Locke's ideas about the importance of a child's early environment. When they looked at the multitude of children crowded into America's slums, they saw a generation at risk. As in England, American reformers tended to combine an exaggerated reverence for the middle-class family with a contemptuous attitude toward the real-life families of the urban poor, which in America was generally synonymous with immigrants. Among the well-to-do, these impoverished immigrants

were sometimes referred to as the "dangerous classes."

In their fight to "rescue" the children of the "dangerous classes," American reformers in the 19th century made use of a powerful weapon: *parens patriae*. A legal doctrine, *parens patriae*—the notion that the state is ultimately the parent of every child—gave officials the authority to remove children from their families if their biological parents were judged unfit.

Parens patriae had existed in America from colonial times, having been borrowed from the English, who considered the king "the father of his country" and acknowledged his authority within his realm to protect those who could not protect themselves. In colonial America, however, *parens patriae* authority was exercised only rarely. In 1745, for example, the Massachusetts Assembly ordered that any child older than six

A young boy holds his baby sister as a woman approaches to take them away. In the major cities of the East, self-proclaimed "child savers" often removed poor children from their homes under the legal doctrine that the state is the ultimate parent of every child and must intervene when parents are unfit.

In the idealized middle-class family of the Victorian era, childhood was viewed as an idyllic time of complete separation from the adult world. For poor families, of course, the need to put food on the table made that impossible. Here children toil in a spinning mill.

who did not know the alphabet be removed from his or her family and placed with another. But this was very much the exception.

Likewise, in the first decades after the United States gained independence from England, *parens patriae* authority existed mainly as a theory. State legislatures had the power to determine when officials could intervene in a family to protect a child's welfare—ample authority to help abused and neglected children—but there was no sense that any problem existed. In the realm of the family, the father—as had been the case throughout most of Western history—remained king.

That began to change—at least for the "dangerous classes"—when immigrants started flooding America's shores and settling in its cities. Initially, concerns centered on saving immigrant children from a life of criminality. In 1825, the nation's first reform school opened in New York City with the goal of teaching delinquent boys a trade and instilling in them "middle-class" values, such as the work ethic. This was to be achieved by contracting out the young lawbreakers' labor to local manufacturers. Perhaps the lessons would have been learned more readily had the working conditions been better—the manufacturers used the youths as a cheap source of unskilled labor, making no real effort to teach them a trade—and had the school's superintendent not kept all of his charges' wages for himself. Ultimately the school failed because the boys constantly ran away. But reformers didn't necessarily see this as evidence that the idea was bad, only that the boys had been too old to be saved. Other efforts concentrated on redeeming younger children.

It wasn't until the 1870s, however, that a case emerged that would focus attention on the issues of child abuse and neglect within the family and lead to a dramatic change in the legal status of children. The case involved Mary Ellen Wilson, an eight-year-old orphan in New York City, who complained to a charity worker of being whipped and beaten daily by her foster family. Malnourished, with cuts and bruises all over her body, Mary Ellen seemed a good candidate for protection by the state. In spite of this, the charity worker searched in vain for a judge who would remove the girl from her foster family. Under the law, children still had no rights per se, and their treatment within the realm of the family was still viewed as the exclusive prerogative of their parents.

Mary Ellen's plight eventually caught the attention of Henry Bergh, founder of the American Society for the Prevention of Cruelty to Animals (ASPCA). The ASPCA brought the case to court, where its lawyers posed a simple question: don't children deserve at least the same protection given to animals? Yes, the judge decided, removing Mary Ellen to a state home and sentencing her foster mother to a jail term.

For the first time, it was suggested that American children might actually have some rights, that there were limits to how their parents could treat them. Just what those rights and limits were—and when the state should intervene to protect children—remained to be definitively answered. In the wake of Mary Ellen Wilson's case, however, child crusaders pushed for widespread intervention, liberally using the *parens patriae* doctrine as justification.

In 1874, as a result of the Wilson case, the New York Society for the Prevention of Cruelty to Children (SPCC) was formed. SPCC chapters were soon operating in every state, and throughout the 1870s and 1880s, many similar groups developed across the country. Unfortunately, despite their names, the goals of these original child-protection groups were often questionable. The emphasis was not on protecting children from abuse but on protecting them from poverty and, by implication, from their unfit parents. "To create the true home," one charity leader explained in 1888, "it was often necessary to break-up the unworthy families." To the middle- and upper-class crusaders, unworthy was roughly synonymous with poor. It didn't seem to occur to anyone that poor parents might genuinely love and be loved by their children, and that those familial bonds might be as important to a child's happiness and emotional well-being as material comforts.

In cities like New York and Boston, self-proclaimed "child-savers," aided by social workers and police, collected poor children and loaded them onto trains bound for the Midwest. There they would work on farms. Away from the squalor of their urban ghettos, the children, it was assumed, would blossom. In many cases what happened was quite different. Upon disembarking from the trains many children were auctioned off to farmers as cheap labor. Rarely did reformers bother to investigate the farm conditions.

Conditions in the reform schools, public homes, and orphanages where other poor children were sent also frequently left much to be desired. In time, reports of scandalous mistreatment of children at these institutions would rock Americans' faith in *parens patriae* solutions to the problem of protecting children.

In 1899, however, the United States would witness the most significant and enduring application of the *parens patriae* doctrine. In that year, Cook County, Illinois, established the first juvenile court. The court's mandate was twofold: to deal with juvenile delinquency and to make custody decisions in cases of abuse and neglect. Other jurisdictions quickly followed suit, and soon nearly every state had set up a juvenile court system.

The distinctive feature of the juvenile courts was their divergence from the rules that applied in the regular courts. Whereas various procedural safeguards protected the rights of defendants in adult courts, juvenile court proceedings were conducted without lawyers, without a jury, without rules of evidence, and typically without a written record. The goal was to avoid stigmatizing the children and their parents, but another effect was to give judges virtually unlimited discretion in deciding cases. And there was no appeal. Social workers also had enormous influence in the system, as it was they who investigated suspected abuse and neglect and gathered the information upon which judges based their decisions.

Although the juvenile courts were supposedly doing what was in the best interest of each child, in the view of many scholars the same class-based biases that plagued earlier *parens patriae* efforts pervaded the juvenile courts. Judges and social workers, who came

Up until the 1960s, child abuse was popularly assumed to exist only among the poor; families such as the one shown here were thought to be immune from the problem. Today we know that abuse can occur in any family, even a well-to-do, high-status one.

predominantly from the middle class, continued to see child abuse and neglect as a problem of the poor. Rarely did the courts break up well-to-do families in the name of a child's welfare.

Even while the juvenile courts were making the state a surrogate parent for increasing numbers of children, however, an opposing trend began to emerge. That trend was exemplified by the first White House Conference on Children, held in 1909. Conference participants—reacting, perhaps, to reports of mistreatment of children in orphanages and public homes—reached the conclusion that even a bad family could be made better than the best institution. Still, the emphasis was on protecting children from the all-encompassing evil of poverty, which obviously meant that child-welfare concerns would focus on the lower classes. There was as yet no sense that child abuse and neglect were major problems, and certainly no official recognition that middle- and upper-class children might need to be protected from abuse or neglect.

That would change only with the 1962 publication of "The Battered Child Syndrome," a research report by Dr. C. Henry Kempe and colleagues. In an age when medical authorities are granted considerable prestige, the qualification of the problem as a syndrome earned it instant recognition and acceptance. Through their report Dr. Kempe and his coauthors finally brought the "safety" of the middle-class family into question. The study suggested that women and children of all classes and races were being mistreated in their own homes.

Even after attention created by publication of "The Battered Child Syndrome," the apparently clear-cut goal of preventing child abuse through regulation and legislation continued to be complicated, as issues of family privacy and parental rights were called into question. Many claimed that the Child Abuse Prevention and Treatment Act of 1974 went too far and was unwarranted federal intrusion into family privacy.

Others claimed that liberal definitions of child abuse were so broad that they denied families' fundamental rights of discipline and self-regulation. Spanking a child in public, for example, could be—and sometimes was—construed as child abuse. Some educators expressed similar concerns, claiming to be hamstrung by the prohibition of corporal punishment as a way of controlling students' behavior.

But legislators sent mixed signals regarding child abuse. The 1980 Federal Adoption Assistance and Child Welfare Act required states to make reasonable efforts to prevent removal of maltreated children from parental custody. This was a return to the belief stated at the 1909 White House Conference on Children—that even a bad family was better than the best institution.

The last decades of the 20th century have been marked by demands for affordable, quality care for children, a demonstration of the changing pattern of family. The parallel interest of lawmakers was demonstrated when the 1997 White House Conference on Children posed the need for affordable, quality child care as a central theme, signaling the attention now focused on children's issues at the national level. In accord with this, state lawmakers are constantly at work on legislation surrounding child abuse and neglect. Despite many seemingly obvious examples of children in crisis, the situation remains tangled and open to interpretation as lawmakers and experts weigh vying opinions on parental rights and custody, family privacy, and what constitutes reasonable effort to protect children.

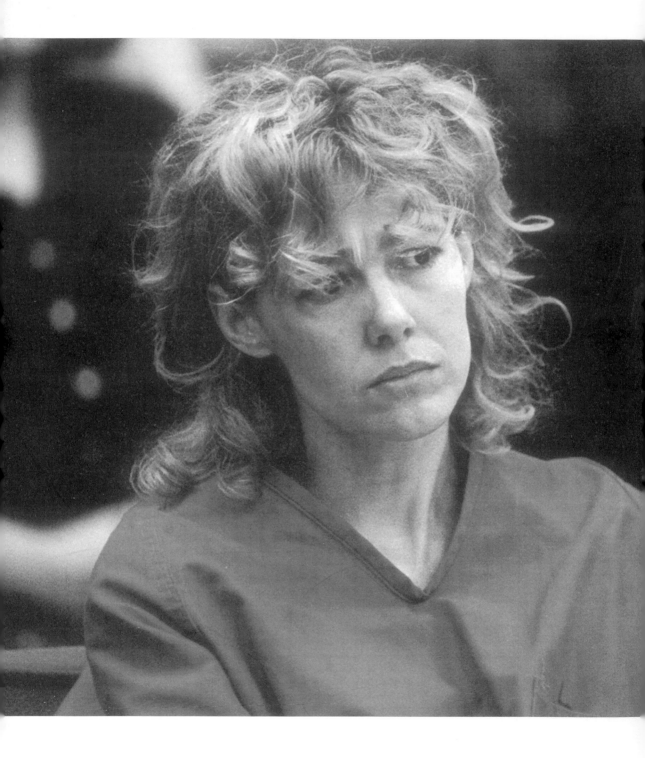

WHO ARE THE ABUSERS?

When child abuse is brought to the attention of the public the first question is, "Who could have committed such a crime?" On one hand the answer is anyone, as an abuser can be of either sex and any race, age, or economic position. Dr. Kempe's 1962 description of the battered child syndrome was the first crack in the stereotypical picture of abuse. Until then physical abuse and neglect had largely been limited to scenarios of poverty, and sexual abuse to the domain of "dirty old men." The truth is that not everyone of similar economic circumstances or personal histories becomes an abuser. As a result the question "Why does someone abuse?" becomes more important than the question "Who abuses?" An answer

Most people's image of a child sex offender wouldn't include Mary Kay LeTourneau (at left), an award-winning elementary school teacher and mother of four. Nevertheless, LeTourneau was sentenced to seven and a half years in prison for having sex with a 13-year-old former student.

Trash surrounds a West Virginia mobile home where an infant was attacked in his crib by rats. Was this neglect or simply the result of poverty? Caseworkers often confront such difficult questions.

to that question may one day help prevent abuse and aid in the development of appropriate punishment or correctional treatment for abusers.

Just as stereotypes surrounding who abuses have been overturned, the idea that abuse stems from a single cause—anger, poverty, or a personal history of abuse—has also changed in favor of the view that child maltreatment is the outgrowth of multiple factors. While it remains important to resist stereotyping, three categories of influence can be used to examine the differences, and similarities, among perpetrators. These categories are as follows:

- the nature of the abuser
- the abuser's family relations
- ,the environment in which the abuser lives and works

Two categories further separate the individual nature of those who abuse. The first category describes abusers who commit acts of commission (defined by what they do), including physical and sexual assault. The second category describes abusers who commit acts of omission (defined by what they don't do), including psychological abuse and neglect. While parents who fail to provide emotional comfort, food, clothing, and shelter are as guilty of abuse as are those who physically assault their children, the two types of abusers are not necessarily interchangeable. Studies have shown that neglectful parents are not destined to become abusive ones. Similarly, abusive parents are not necessarily neglectful. A case involving two elementary school children in Kentucky demonstrates this and points to the way an understanding of the three categories of influence may be used in evaluating the motives of the abuser and therefore in determining the extent to which a child is at risk of additional harm.

When Rose Hartman, an elementary school teacher in central Kentucky, brought two of her students to see the school nurse, she was concerned that only one of the children, Mitch, was suffering from parental maltreatment. The other child, Brenda, simply needed a cut rebandaged. Aged nine, Mitch appeared and acted much younger than his classmates. He wore the same faded jeans and T-shirt every day, avoided interaction with other children, and often fell asleep at his desk. Already concerned, Mrs. Hartman became alarmed when the rail-thin Mitch was accused of stealing food from a classmate's lunchbox. After Mitch's mother missed a scheduled parent-teacher conference, Mrs. Hartman decided to seek the professional advice of a colleague. When a bandage fell off Brenda's arm during recess, Mrs. Hartman asked Mitch to accompany them to the school nurse, hoping not to attract attention to his problems.

On the surface Brenda was strikingly different from Mitch. Although they were the same age, Brenda stood a head taller, was vivacious, and interacted easily with other children. Always neatly dressed in colorful clothing with designer labels, Brenda readily assumed a leadership role among her classmates, sorting out playground trouble and excelling in schoolwork. Mrs. Hartman also knew Brenda's parents and during parent-teacher conferences had laughingly acknowledged Brenda's mother's rueful remark about the number of times Brenda's high energy had gotten her into scrapes that resulted in cuts, bruises, and even a broken arm. Mrs. Hartman was shocked when the school nurse, after examining and speaking with Mitch and Brenda separately, said that she wanted to talk to the Department of Social Services about both children. Interviews between representatives of the Department of Social Services and the parents of Mitch and Brenda revealed characteristics of abuse and neglect.

Mitch Renfro was the oldest of three children being raised by a single mother. When interviewed by social workers, Ms. Renfro said that it was very important that her children not live in the public housing project where she had grown up. Because of this, she had taken a second job to afford the move to a house in a suburban neighborhood. She added proudly that it was only Mitch's willingness to help that made their improved living situation possible. Because her work schedule required her to be away from home much of the day and evening, Mitch prepared meals for the other children, bathed and dressed all of them, and helped keep the house clean. When social workers asked why she had not attended a parent-teacher conference, she explained that she couldn't afford to take time off from work. The social workers quickly realized that Ms. Renfro's intentions were good, but her personal history and current financial problems were clouding her judgment. She simply didn't see the damage being done to her small children.

Social workers looked at three major influences before determining that Mitch and his siblings could remain with their mother and not suffer additional harm. First, they determined that Ms. Renfro exhibited no violent tendencies or sudden mood swings and that her manner of child care, although below standard, was consistent. Second, while Ms. Renfro admitted that her father had physically abused her as a child, she was actively trying to break this cycle by moving her children away from their potentially abusive grandfather. Unfortunately, her background didn't provide her with an adequate knowledge of parenting skills—perhaps the main factor in her misjudgment of Mitch's ability to undertake responsibilities beyond his age level. And third, Ms. Renfro was creating a new life for herself and her family through her positive involvement at work and her willingness to receive help when offered. While she was certainly guilty of acts of omission, she didn't appear likely to commit acts of commission. With help understanding her children's needs and instruction in hygiene, nutrition, and child development, Ms. Renfro seemed a good candidate to break the cycle of neglect and was considered at no risk of becoming abusive.

After the school nurse decided that the injuries under Brenda's bandage didn't look accidental, social workers visited her parents and found a tragedy waiting to happen. Brenda Miller's parents were very different from Mitch Renfro's mother. Brenda's father worked in a high-pressure job as a stockbroker; her mother was active in charitable organizations. Both were well known as involved parents.

Despite outward signs of a happy, supportive family, social workers noticed that when asked about the cause of Brenda's injuries her father was quick to say, "Brenda is always in the way." The social workers immediately became concerned and investigated further. They found that Brenda's father translated the pressures he felt at work into violence at home, routinely blaming Brenda's need for attention as the cause of his problems. While remorseful for any injuries that might have occurred, Mr. Miller did not blame himself. Instead he stated that Brenda needed "to learn to behave and stay out of the way."

For her part, Brenda's mother said that she would work harder to keep Brenda away from her father when he was tired. She revealed that her own father had also been "overworked." Social workers felt that this clue to Mrs. Miller's history was important, as her past might prevent her from realizing that even occasional violence precipitated by pressure is abuse. In addition, the family enjoyed enormous prestige in the community, and it was unlikely that either Mrs. Miller or Brenda would speak out against what was happening because of a combination of guilt and their conditioning to "protect the family name." Nor was it likely that Mr. Miller would admit that he needed help controlling his temper. As a result, social workers continued to visit the home routinely and made sure the Millers understood that evidence of continued physical abuse might result in a court order removing Brenda to foster care.

Contrasted with the case findings in the neglect of the Keystone kids and the abuse of Elisa Izquierdo, similarities and differences between the abusers become clearer. As individuals, the mothers of the Keystone kids had drug problems, which impaired their ability to make decisions. They also had no history of a desire to change their behavior. Furthermore, they were acting as a neglectful family unit, cutting themselves off from outside contact and creating an

In single-parent and two-career households in which children spend much time on their own, parents must consider whether the responsibilities they give their kids are age appropriate.

environment in which a pattern of neglect could continue and get worse. Caseworkers believed that the high level of neglect placed the Keystone kids at immediate risk of disease and malnutrition if they were left in the care of their mothers.

Similarly, Elisa Izquierdo's mother was prone to violent mood swings and had distanced herself from other adults who were concerned about Elisa. In the wake of media attention surrounding Elisa's death, many experts pointed to the number of indicators present in

Living room of a South Side apartment, Chicago. Poverty and overcrowding are risk factors for child abuse, but American courts have ruled that poverty alone cannot justify breaking up a family.

Elisa's mother's behavior, her relationship with family, and her connection with the community and were outraged that the New York Child Welfare Administration had not intervened. The fact that Elisa remained with her mother despite substantial warning signs indicates how difficult it is to recognize not only abuse but also the level of imminent danger the abuser presents.

Just as those who neglect or physically abuse cannot be neatly categorized, sexual abusers also come from a variety of backgrounds. In February 1997 police in Seattle, Washington, had to adjust their image of a sexual perpetrator to include attractive, educated Mary Kay LeTourneau. Married, and the mother of four young children, LeTourneau was an award-winning elementary school teacher. The entire country was shocked when she was convicted of second-degree child rape for having a sexual relationship (and baby) with a former student, a 13-year-old boy. LeTourneau was sentenced to seven and a half years in prison, but her story didn't end there.

Six months into her sentence she was released on the condition that she never contact the young man again. A few weeks later, in early February of 1998, police discovered Mary Kay LeTourneau in a gray Volkswagen Fox parked on a residential street. The car's parking lights were on, its windows steamed. More important, the young man she was forbidden to contact was sitting beside her. Having broken the terms of her release, and now considered at risk of being a repeat offender, LeTourneau was returned to prison to serve the remainder of her sentence.

Sexual abuse, while sometimes accompanied by physical abuse, is less likely than physical abuse to be triggered by economic disadvantage. As the case of Mary Kay LeTourneau shows, it is wrong to stereotype sexual offenders. However, it remains true that most sexual offenders are older men, with a smaller number of adolescent or female perpetrators.

Research shows that sexual abuse may be divided into two broad groups: extrafamilial (involving a perpetrator outside the family) and incestuous (involving a perpetrator within the family). Mary Kay LeTourneau's relationship with her 13-year-old former student is an example of extrafamilial sexual abuse. Another famous example occurred in 1994, when seven-year-old Megan Kanka was sexually assaulted and murdered by a neighbor. Extrafamilial sexual crimes may also include improper fondling, flashing, child pornography, and obscene phone calls. Much debate exists around why these crimes are committed, and few definitive answers exist. However, most extrafamilial sexual crimes are felt to center on the perpetrator's desire to fulfill a specific sexual need, combined with the lack of social skills necessary to obtain sex within the perpetrator's peer group. Obviously these characteristics alone do not create a sexual abuser. Experts are calling for more research to identify other risk factors.

Incestuous sexual abuse is felt to stem from a separate set of needs. Most instances, although certainly not all, involve a father, stepfather, or uncle. At the heart of the problem lies not sex but the need for power and control. Experts cite a variety of possible triggers, which combine with aspects of the abuser's individual history, family relations, and involvement with the community to put him at risk. The triggers and risk factors include the following family characteristics:

- habitual absence of either the mother or father
- assignment of a "mother" role (for example, cooking or caring for other children) to a daughter
- presence of a stepparent or live-in boyfriend
- history of child abuse in one or both parents
- overcrowded living conditions
- history of alcoholism or drug abuse in one or both parents
- inability to establish normal social conditions outside the family because of an eccentric belief system, extreme poverty, or the remoteness of the area in which the family lives

In many cases of physical abuse or neglect, the court system leaves a child with his or her biological parents in exchange for the promise of corrected behavior (as in the case of Elisa Izquierdo). This happens far less often in cases involving sexual abuse. Sexual acts outside the parameters society has established by custom and law have always been strongly censured, with little margin for leniency. When detected, they almost always result in intervention by the court system.

Of course, "when detected" is the operative phrase. Many cases of child abuse—whether sexual abuse, physical abuse, or neglect—never come to the attention of the authorities. In fact, actual incidents are believed to exceed reported ones by 100 percent or more. Obviously, this cannot put parents' minds at ease. Nor can the media attention lavished on the worst cases of abuse (or suspected abuse). But some observers would say that concern about child abuse has in recent years reached the level of near-hysteria. There is a sense that potential abusers lurk everywhere and that we're not doing enough to protect our children. Unfortunately, this moral panic has only been compounded by economic and social changes in American society.

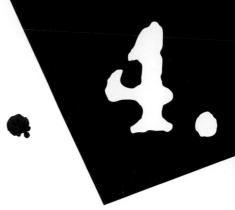

WHO IS
WATCHING
THE CHILDREN?

I n 1970, according to the Bureau of Labor Statistics, only 28.7 percent of American mothers with children under the age of six were in the workforce. By 1990 that number had doubled, to 58.2 percent, and a continued rise was projected. Simultaneously, an increasingly mobile society has dispersed extended families, significantly reducing the number of children being cared for by relatives. And the number of single-parent families has grown steadily, today representing one in every five children.

The result has been an unprecedented need for day care. At the very time this need is greatest, however, fear of child abuse looms largest. In deciding whether to put their children in a commercial, nonprofit, or home-based care facility, parents must confront not only the question of whether their children's developmental needs will be met but also a much more terrible and fundamental question: will their children be safe from physical and sexual abuse?

Who is watching the children? The answer, increasingly, is someone other than their parents. Social and economic changes in America have led to a great need for day care.

51

Safe, quality day care has concerned public officials as well, and various regulations now govern the child care industry. Facilities are periodically inspected, and workers in day care centers must undergo criminal background checks. Still, fears about child abuse in day care remain high.

To a certain extent, these fears may be misplaced. According to a study for the United States National Center of Child Abuse and Neglect, children are less likely to be abused by day care workers than they are by their own parents. This is not to say that problems do not exist at child care facilities, however.

Barbara Daniels and her husband wanted their six-and-a-half-month-old daughter to receive individual attention, so they chose a day care provider who would keep their daughter in her home. However, on only the fourth day of this arrangement, a problem arose. Barbara arrived at the caregiver's home and found her daughter screaming hysterically and sweating profusely. When she noticed that her daughter's right leg was swollen, Barbara took the baby to a hospital emergency room. There doctors told her that the swelling was caused by a twisting break known as a spiral fracture—a strong indication of abuse. Barbara and her husband immediately removed their daughter from child care forever.

Incidents of child abuse such as the Daniels case often find their way into news reports. This is particularly true when the abuse occurs in a day care setting, because then multiple, unrelated children may be affected. The result of all the news reports may be to produce a sense of moral panic.

Yet the real threat of child abuse might be somewhat overblown by the news media. Media scholars have noted that, in general, violent crime tends to receive disproportionate news coverage, giving people the impression that their world is more dangerous than it really is. If, for example, a metropolitan area of 5 million people has 300 murders during a typical year, statistically the chances of being a murder victim are extremely slim. But if murders are consistently the lead stories on nightly news broadcasts, and if they consistently receive front-page coverage in the newspapers, over time people may come to feel their lives are in imminent peril. A similar phenomenon may be at work with child abuse. As the media focus a great deal of attention on violent predators or abuse within child care facilities, many people, particularly parents, may fear that child abusers are lurking everywhere.

No incident illustrates the power of the media to whip up hysteria over child abuse—or demonstrates how moral panic can grip a community, even the entire nation—better than the McMartin Preschool case. On August 12, 1983, Judy Johnson complained to police in Manhattan Beach, California, that her two-year-old son had been molested at the McMartin Preschool by Ray Buckey, a part-time aide. Buckey's mother, Peggy, and his grandmother, Virginia McMartin, owned the child care center. Buckey was arrested in early September, but the district attorney decided that there wasn't enough evidence to prosecute.

Before long, however, Manhattan Beach's chief of police had sent out a letter to parents of current and former students at McMartin Preschool. The letter informed the parents that Buckey may have sexually abused their children and requested that parents question their kids about any incidents. Although the letter was supposed to be confidential, a local TV station got wind of the story and was soon reporting that McMartin Preschool might be linked with a child-pornography and prostitution ring. The media frenzy was on.

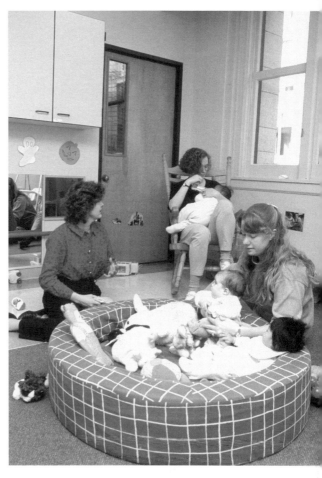

Statistically, children are much less likely to be abused in a day care setting than they are at home. But society's fears largely focus on child care providers.

Over the next seven years, as events in Manhattan Beach took a series of bizarre turns, the McMartin case became a national news obsession. Virtually every major newspaper and newsmagazine, supplemented by nightly news broadcasts and TV newsmagazines such as *20/20* and *Nightline*, closely reported the unfolding story.

Initially, frightened parents asked therapists to discover exactly what had happened to their children. Investigators concluded that as many as 369 of the 400 children they interviewed had been abused over a 10-year period. And the abuse was extremely chilling. Children told of being forced to pose for pornographic photos and act in pornographic films. Some said they'd been taken to a cemetery and buried in a coffin. Many kids described being led through trapdoors in their classrooms to secret underground tunnels where McMartin Preschool workers sexually abused them. (Distraught parents excavated the ground around the center in a fruitless effort to find these tunnels.) Some children even told therapists and social workers that they had witnessed Satanic rituals, such as the mutilation and killing of animals and the murder of infant humans whose blood was then drunk.

All these horrors, and many more, were reported extensively in the media. As a result, McMartin Preschool became the embodiment of every working parent's worst nightmare. If such terrible abuse could happen at this little preschool near the beach, with its elderly matriarch and kind- and motherly-looking teachers, couldn't it happen at any day care center?

But had the terrible acts children described actually taken place at McMartin? Indeed, had *any* abuse taken place? These questions don't seem to have been seriously considered—by news organizations or concerned parents—until after the legal process had finally run its course.

In March 1984, prosecutors filed more than 200 criminal counts, including rape, sodomy, and child

pornography charges, against day care owners Virginia McMartin and Peggy Buckey, aide Ray Buckey, and four teachers. (Eventually more than 320 charges would be filed.) In January 1986, following 17 months of preliminary hearings, lack of evidence forced prosecutors to drop the charges against all the defendants except Peggy and Ray Buckey. In January 1990, following a three-year-long trial, a jury acquitted Peggy Buckey of all charges. The jury also found Ray Buckey not guilty on 39 of the 52 counts he faced, and the judge dismissed an additional charge. Jurors deadlocked on 12 remaining counts of child molestation. A retrial on those 12 counts again resulted in a hung jury, and prosecutors decided to drop the case against Buckey.

One of the longest and costliest criminal cases in California history was over, and not a single conviction had been obtained. Still, many parents—and much of

Peggy Buckey, co-owner of the McMartin Preschool child care center, listens to opening statements during her trial for child abuse and molestation, July 13, 1987. The McMartin case fanned hysteria about child abuse but ultimately resulted in no convictions.

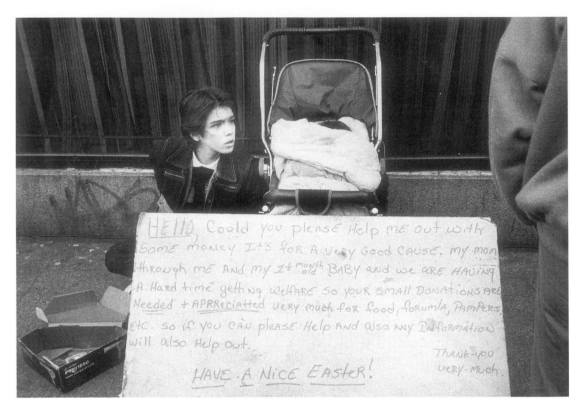

HELLO, Could you pleasE HelP mE out with some moneY It's for A vERy Good CAUSE. my mom through mE And my 2ᵗ month old BABY and we are HAUING A Hard time getting welfARE so your small DONATIONS ARE Needed + APRReciAtted very much for food, forumlA, PAmPers, Etc. so if you cAn pleasE Help And also Any InformAtion will also Help out.

HAVE A NiCE EAsteR!

THANK-you
very-much

Homelessness, out-of-wedlock births, and teenage mothers are some of the factors that tend to put children at risk.

the news media—continued to portray the McMartin defendants as abusers who had escaped on legal technicalities. Other observers disagreed, pointing out that the investigatory techniques of police and social workers, especially the leading questions that had been asked of the children, were deeply flawed because they assumed that the abuse had occurred. (Testimonial issues regarding children will be discussed in more depth in the next chapter.)

Whatever the truth of the matter, the McMartin case exacted a tremendous toll on the defendants, the children and their parents, and the community. The defendants racked up huge legal bills and saw their reputations ruined. Peggy Buckey spent two years in jail before being released on bail; bail was denied her son Ray, who spent the years 1984 through 1989 behind bars. The children's repeated testimony about the real or imagined horrors they endured caused some observers to remark that if they hadn't been abused before the trials, the children certainly were by the end. Their parents, of course, had to live with the terrible uncertainty and with feelings of guilt. And the community as a whole seemed exhausted by the protracted ordeal.

Despite the unanswered questions, child care experts cite several lessons that may be learned from the McMartin case:

- While parents should be aware of the possibility of child abuse, the threat must not be exaggerated. Keeping a watchful eye for signs of abuse is a reasonable response; being fearful and suspicious of everyone is not.
- Children should be encouraged to tell about sexual abuse without fear of punishment. At the same time, however, when there is a suspicion of abuse, great care must be exercised in how children are asked about their experiences. As terrible as the sexual exploitation of children is, it must be remembered that false accusations of child abuse can also do terrible harm to adults.

Sadly, as custody of children is less likely to be routinely assigned to the mother in cases of divorce, false accusations of child abuse sometimes stem from one parent's desire to have sole custody of a child. Attorneys and judges are becoming savvy about verifying the truth. As one divorce attorney says, "A parent who decides their spouse is abusing the children and sues for divorce is one matter. When a divorce case is almost settled and sole or joint custody is awarded to one parent and the other suddenly screams child abuse I have become suspect."

The same moral panic that leads parents to distrust child care workers, Scout leaders, even ministers and priests, has affected social workers. The decision to place children in foster care and eventually to move forward with adoption is influenced not only by legislation but by the media attention given to cases such as that of Elisa Izquierdo, in which foster care would have saved a life.

On the other hand, some feel that the decision to place a child in foster care has significant drawbacks. Certainly it may have a destabilizing effect on the child. "Foster care, intended to protect children who are abused and neglected by their parents, is too often an equally cruel form of abuse and neglect," stated the National Commission of Children in a report on the needs of the nation's children issued in June of 1991. This was in response to the 1980 federal law aimed at putting children into more-permanent family situations. The opinion that foster care can be another form of abuse and neglect is not necessarily a statement about the level of care in foster homes. Rather, it is an acknowledgment that when children are moved from home to home without a sense of permanence, the effect can be as disorienting as the poor care they were receiving from their biological family. Negative attitudes surrounding foster care can also affect a child's self-esteem.

By the time Max Moran turned 21 and left the New York City foster care program, he had spent six years in group homes. Commenting on his experience, he said, "When somebody found out I was in a group home, the first question was always, 'What did you do?' like I broke the law and that was my punishment, to be put into a group home."

In response to these problems, states like Kentucky are attempting to speed up the decision-making process regarding not only removal of a child to foster care but the permanent removal of children from their biological parents. The goal is to have a permanent family in mind when the decision is made to terminate the rights of the biological parents. While perhaps an unattainable goal,

it demonstrates the importance states are placing on the permanence of the place a child calls home. In a slightly different approach, some jurisdictions in Ohio are seeking to develop neighborhood-based foster care—foster families and services located in the neighborhoods where most of the children who enter foster care come from. This, it is hoped, will reduce the disruption that foster care placement causes in the children's lives. "These kids need to maintain friendships and whatever sense of security we can give them," say promoters of the plan. Clearly, all of these concerns are related to the larger realization that the safety of the children is the most important factor in any decision.

This interest in finding not only safe but permanent homes for endangered children has placed adoption as the top priority for children who must be removed from their biological parents. Hoping to counteract some of

A toddler is taken to her new foster home. While everyone concedes that placing a child in foster care is preferable to having the child abused at home, foster care is not without major drawbacks.

the long-term effects of abuse by providing a stable emotional as well as physical environment, the Clinton administration proposed a major child welfare initiative: a plan to double, by the year 2002, the number of children who were placed in adoption in 1997. This was quite an ambitious goal, as in 1997 the number of children adopted from foster care was 20,000.

While social workers strive to keep children with their biological families, the number of children considered at risk unless removed to foster care continues to rise. There is wide agreement that the crisis is linked to increases in the following:

- number of reported cases of child neglect and abuse
- alcohol and drug abuse, particularly abuse of crack cocaine
- AIDS cases and the number of children born exposed to HIV, many of whom are abandoned at birth
- number of children born to teenage girls
- number of children born to unmarried women
- number of homeless children and children living in poverty

No one pretends a numbers game can solve all problems associated with foster care and adoption. The most important step continues to be identifying which children, like the Keystone kids, need to be removed from their parents, and which, like Mitch Renfro, can stay. It is for this reason that states such as Kentucky have created two legal tracks for the protection of children from abuse. The first track is the more traditional criminal trial of the offender. However, the fear that this may leave the child under the continued direct care and supervision of the accused has made the second track equally important in the eyes of child welfare experts. The second track, which is termed a Dependency and Neglect Proceeding, has been created to allow authorities to remove a child from the care of the accused, independent of the conclusion of the criminal trial. Significantly, it allows a different burden of proof to determine the future of the child's physical relationship to the accused. While a criminal proceeding is a trial by jury and follows all legal aspects of evidence and burden of proof, the Dependency and Neglect Proceeding is adjudicated by a judge, and hearsay is admissible as evidence. This lowered standard of proof is aimed entirely at quickly protecting children from future harm.

It is important to understand the damage done by poor decision making in either direction. Most obvious is the child who remains with a parent and is permanently injured or killed, like Elisa Izquierdo. However, the moral panic created by fatalities like Elisa can create a vacuum in which social workers overreact, removing children from parents with little supporting evidence. The break this creates in a family and the emotional damage it does to both parents and children may also be irreparable. Unfortunately this is the reality of the decisions that affect the lives of children every day around the country.

AGE MATTERS

While physical abuse is criminal regardless of the victim's age, 20th-century American society—and the judicial system—places particular emphasis on protecting children. Laws assume that children are less able than adults to defend themselves physically and less able to judge the long-term repercussions of their decisions. But the very youth of children, which forms the basis for society's belief that they need special protection, also complicates actual efforts to protect them. Quite simply, given children's limited experience and verbal abilities, along with their suggestibility and supposedly active imaginations, adults often don't know when to believe and when to disbelieve a child's story of abuse—or at least how to interpret the details—particularly if the child is very young.

The special status of children led to the creation of a legal term for them: minors. Most often, this legal status comes into play when a child is accused of a

A social worker interviews a five-year-old boy in a case of suspected child abuse. Though young children are capable of recalling events with great accuracy, careless or overzealous interviewing techniques can obscure the truth and make a child's testimony worthless.

crime—by mandating special rules within the legal proceedings and limiting the minor's responsibility and
punishment. But the legal status of a minor can also
play a role when the child is the victim. This was illus-
trated in the arrest and conviction of Mary Kay
LeTourneau. Even after LeTourneau was sent to prison,
her 13-year-old victim claimed that he had willingly
agreed to sexual relations with her and loved her just as
she claimed to love him. That was irrelevant to the
case, however. Under the law, a minor cannot be a willing participant in a sexual act with an adult because the
minor presumably can't fully understand the long-term
consequences of his or her actions. Therefore
LeTourneau, as the adult participant, was criminally
responsible despite mutual claims of love on the part of
victim and offender.

In the realm of child abuse, another important issue
has recently come to the forefront regarding the status
of minors in the courtroom: children's testimony.
Specifically, what provisions should be made for a child
to testify in court, and how reliable should a child's
testimony be considered? Historically, courtroom testimony by children was not only viewed as inherently
unreliable but also discouraged because of the emotional ordeal it presented for the young witnesses. In
the 1980s, however, this began to change.

Increasingly social workers, law enforcement
authorities, and parents have been encouraged to give
more credence to a child's claim of abuse. Child welfare
experts view this as a positive trend and hope that maltreated children will receive protection and help as
they bring their story to the attention of authorities.

The legal system, too, has become more willing
to accept children's testimony in the courtroom.
Procedures have been adapted to accommodate children's special needs. In some states, for example,
judges step down from the bench and abandon their
robes to make children more at ease. Many states have

passed laws permitting young children to testify over closed-circuit television if they are afraid to appear in the courtroom with the accused. Other states accept videotaped testimony.

While most people applaud the efforts to obtain the testimony of abused children—and to do so in a manner that protects them from further emotional trauma—some observers worry that overzealous or careless interviewers may skew or misinterpret children's stories. In the absence of the more-rigorous procedures used to test the validity of adults' testimony, these observers feel, there is a greater risk that innocent people may be arrested, tried, and convicted for crimes

A defense attorney questions a nine-year-old who accused her father of abuse, 1958. Historically the testimony of young children was considered inherently unreliable.

Using a doll, a psychologist interviews two girls about sexual abuse. Dolls may help young children demonstrate what happened to them, avoiding potential confusion about anatomical terms. But some experts believe that the use of dolls may also distort children's stories.

they didn't commit. So although children's allegations must always be taken seriously, moral panic must not be allowed to diminish the good judgment of adults.

The issue is most crucial in cases of alleged sexual abuse because those cases often lack the physical evidence (malnourishment, broken bones, cuts, bruises, burns) and corroborating witnesses (doctors, teachers, neighbors) that are present in many cases of physical abuse and neglect. This is especially true in cases of flashing, fondling, or improper verbal suggestions.

Uncovering and punishing the sexual abuse of children also presents other problems. Older victims may be susceptible to threats from the abuser or may feel too ashamed to report the abuse. Younger children might not understand that what is being done to them is wrong, and they might have difficulty coherently describing their experiences. Often in cases of suspected abuse therapists and social workers are called upon to piece together what has happened, and all they have to go on is what they can elicit from the children. Therein lies a potential problem.

Once again, the McMartin Preschool case serves as a cautionary tale—both for those who generally favor the use of children's testimony and those who think it generally unreliable. Those who believe that the McMartin defendants were unjustly accused claim that in the climate of hysteria that surrounded the case, interviewers accepted that abuse had occurred, and then, consciously or otherwise, set out to uncover the "evidence" to support their predetermined conclusion. Critics note that young children generally want to please adults, and they may be quite attuned to subtle cues that indicate the responses an interviewer is looking for. Researchers have found, for example, that if a child is asked the same question twice in a row, the answer will change—presumably because the child believes the first answer wasn't the "right" one. Critics of the McMartin investigation charge that a host of similarly faulty interview techniques led to the total fabrication of the children's testimony. How else, they ask, can the kids' outlandish stories be explained? Stories, for example, of being flown to Palm Springs in an airplane or hot-air balloon, abused, and then returned to the day care center—all before their parents arrived to pick them up. Stories of getting flushed down toilets and being sexually abused in sewers. Stories of flying witches and dead, burned babies.

On the other hand, those who believe that the McMartin defendants were acquitted in spite of their guilt claim that preschool-age children could never have manufactured such elaborate tales if an element of truth had not been present. These people agree that the interviewers' techniques were flawed, but mainly because they relied on suggestive questions and didn't allow the children to relate their experiences in their own words. After the trials some jurors did say that they believed abuse had occurred at McMartin Preschool, but they simply couldn't rely on the testimony of the children as it had been gathered.

At the core of these concerns lies the suggestibility of children. One researcher who has devoted much effort to educating law enforcement authorities, social workers, and attorneys on avoiding this problem and collecting accurate testimony from children is Stephen Ceci, a developmental psychologist. Ceci's research has been cited in a decision written for the U.S. Court of Appeals involving interview methods used in a sexual abuse case, and the workshops he conducts across the country have been heralded as "eye-opening" by child welfare and law enforcement experts.

Ceci teaches that scientific data often contradicts what attorneys, judges, social workers, and law enforcement authorities are convinced they know from their years of experience. Many interviewers erroneously think they can "read" the truth from a child's facial expressions and body language, which Ceci calls a "Pinocchio Test." (In the story of Pinocchio, the title character's nose grows every time he tells a lie.) "You could toss a coin and do as well as they do," Ceci asserts.

Children have a memory system capable of great accuracy, Ceci believes, but poor interviewing procedures can obscure the truth. Similarly, he maintains that adults—even professional interviewers who take careful notes—are also at risk of having faulty memories. As a result, many experts now advocate the videotaping of all interviews to provide reliable, and unchangeable, documentation.

To eliminate the "Pinocchio Test," which relies on the instincts of an interviewer and his or her emotional connection with the child, Ceci advocates what he terms a scientific approach instead of the traditional confirmatory method. A case of suspected sexual abuse illustrates the pitfalls of the confirmatory method. A

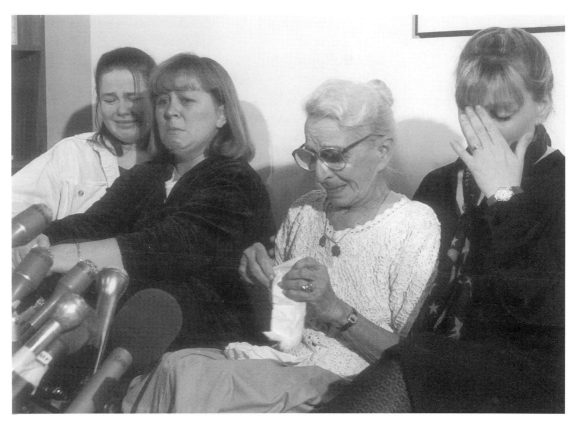

four-year-old girl was left alone one Saturday morning with her mother's boyfriend, Randy. Later that day, after the mother had returned and Randy was gone, the girl told her mother, "Randy put his pee-pee in my pee-pee." The mother immediately called an abuse hotline, and a social worker went to the house. The social worker began the interview by asking confirmatory questions: Where were you? How did it feel? Who else was in the room? Questioners using the scientific approach would have posed a different set of questions: Can you show me pee-pee? What do you mean by pee-pee?

When the child was finally asked the last two questions, she indicated that pee-pee was urine. Quickly the real story unfolded. The child urinated in the toilet and didn't flush. Randy later urinated in the same toilet, "putting his pee-pee in her pee-pee." With this revela-

By the time they held this press conference in 1997 after losing a legal appeal, Violet Amirault (center, wearing glasses) and her daughter Cheryl Amirault LeFave (right) had served nearly a decade behind bars for child sexual abuse at a Massachusetts day care center. The women at left are the wife and daughter of Gerald Amirault, who was also convicted in the case. In 1998 a judge ruled that the original trials had been tainted by flawed interviews of the children.

tion what might have become an embarrassing and potentially tragic situation was quickly shown to be nothing more than a misunderstanding.

Not all child welfare experts advocate the discarding of old techniques, though most would acknowledge the need for greater awareness of the techniques' limitations. Some of the more potentially problematic techniques still in use are

- leading questions
- questions that require only yes or no responses
- anatomically correct dolls
- pretend dialogue

The McMartin case highlights how these techniques can work against obtaining the truth. When, after the first trial, seven of the jurors appeared at a press conference, they stated that the main defect in the prosecution's case was the badgering of the child witnesses by therapists. The jurors had watched videotapes of the interviews and decided that they never "heard the children tell the story in their own words." Instead of scientific questions, which try to disprove a hypothesis, the children were asked confirmatory questions, which buried any hope of a scientific refutation of the original hypothesis.

The two types of questions are easily distinguishable. Scientific questions could include: What did Mr. Buckey do? Where did he do it? Did he do this to anyone else? Did he do this to a policeman? Did he do this to the principal?

Confirmatory questions take many different forms. They could include: When Mr. Buckey touched you, did it hurt? (a leading confirmatory question, which already accepts the fact that "touching" occurred) Do you remember how many times he touched you? (both a confirmatory question and a yes/no response question)

Anatomically correct dolls are also used to encourage children to demonstrate what happened to them. This method may help children who lack the verbal skills necessary to explain what occurred. However, much debate exists over the suggestibility posed by the dolls' exaggerated anatomy.

Pretend dialogue has some of the same drawbacks. It may encourage children who are hesitant to speak about their abuse by engaging them in a nonthreatening manner. However, pretend dialogue may also encourage invention over truth.

Using a combination of these techniques, interviewers in the McMartin case eventually elicited a series of fantastic stories that were unsupported by physical evidence, impossible to substantiate, and, in some cases, in conflict not merely with common sense but with the laws of physics. The children's testimony had become so distorted as to be useless in court. As a result the jurors had no basis upon which to convict.

The lesson, experts say, is that children must be listened to carefully and scientifically. Emotional responses and preconceptions have no place in fact-finding. Scientific questioning not only protects the innocent from being accused, it also protects the validity of a child's testimony.

Just as poor interviewing techniques can prevent accurate testimony from children, so too can fear. Many courts—particularly family courts, which deal primarily in matters related to children and their parents—are modifying physical aspects of the courtroom to make children feel more comfortable. While few people have a problem with judges' removing their robes or stepping down from behind the bench where they usually sit, many defendants are contesting the decision to allow children to testify from another room, with the testimony projected on a screen in the actual courtroom. The purpose, of course, is to spare the child the trauma of a face-to-face confrontation with the defendant. But defendants have maintained that the

Marilyn Van Derbur, Miss America 1958. During the 1980s and 1990s, a host of celebrities, including Van Derbur, claimed they had been sexually abused as children.

arrangement violates their Sixth Amendment right to confront the witnesses against them. However, *Maryland v. Craig* upheld the constitutionality of allowing children to testify from a remote location, provided certain restrictions are met. At a pretrial hearing the child's fear of a face-to-face confrontation with the accused must be demonstrated. Concern that this fear might influence the child's ability to testify truthfully outweighs the objections of defendants.

As courts try to define the limits of a child's testimony and proper place in the courtroom in cases of abuse, another abuse-related testimonial battle has erupted. This one, however, involves not children but adults who suddenly "recover" memories of childhood abuse that they had presumably repressed completely. Recovered memory frequently occurs during therapy, often with the aid of hypnosis.

In the 1980s and 1990s, a spate of victims—including famous figures such as former Miss America Marilyn Van Derbur and comedian Roseanne Barr—came forward with their stories of recovered memories of abuse. This only heightened the nation's fear of child abuse. If victims could go years, perhaps even their entire lives, without even knowing they had been abused, didn't that mean that child abuse was even more underreported than previously assumed? Many states responded to recovered-memory cases by changing existing statutes of limitations to allow accused abusers to be tried despite the number of years between the alleged crimes and the accusations.

At the same time, however, skeptics began questioning the phenomenon of recovered memory. They pointed to certain accusations that were demonstrably false. In 1992, for example, a young woman under the care of a therapist recovered memories of being repeatedly raped by her father, a minister, when she was between the ages of 7 and 14. Twice, she recalled, her father had made her abort her pregnancies with a coat hanger. The accusations ruined her father's reputation, and he was forced to resign his post as a minister. Only later did a medical examination reveal that the woman had never been pregnant; indeed, she was still a virgin.

Critics question the reliability of the methods therapists use to help patients recover childhood memories. One such method is hypnosis. The use of hypnosis to help witnesses remember has been a part of criminal justice for more than three decades. In 1968 the Maryland Supreme Court of Appeals made admissible "refreshed memory." Since then states have set their own guidelines—some allowing hypnotically refreshed testimony only if the hypnotist fulfilled certain procedural guide-lines. The U.S. Supreme Court weighed in on the matter in 1987, when it supported the application of a case-by-case determination of admissibility in its *Rock v. Arkansas* ruling. Despite the conditional acceptance of hypnosis by the legal system, the American Medical Association (AMA) warns that new information gained under hypnosis should be verified independently and that even when essentially accurate it may involve the filling of certain memory gaps with fantasy.

Another technique some therapists use is to have patients imagine childhood events, hoping that this will lead to the recovery of lost memories. In the course of the exercise, the therapist might ask a series of questions: Where did the event happen? When? What was the weather like? Who was with you?

Might such suggestive techniques, particularly when used by careless therapists, instill in patients totally false but confidently held memories of child-hood abuse? Research suggests that they might. In fact, under experimental conditions various researchers have demonstrated how false childhood memories can be planted using some of the same techniques that therapists use to help patients recover memories. What the researchers can't say, however, is that real repressed memories of childhood abuse are never recovered in adulthood. Many medical professionals do, in fact, accept that individuals can lose memories of traumatic childhood events and later recover those memories. What is questioned is the consistency and reliability of the recovered memory, which may be greatly influenced by the current mood of the adult. A person who is depressed or anxious might be especially likely to "recall" memories that are negative or disturbing.

The question, therefore, becomes, how much confidence can the legal system place in recovered memories of childhood abuse? The Philadelphia-based False Memory Syndrome Foundation (FMSF), which was founded in 1992 to combat the wave of accusations and lawsuits brought by victims with recovered memory, believes that a high degree of skepticism should be the rule. FMSF cites problems created by ill-trained therapists who plant false notions in their patients.

Many others claim that a combination of moral panic and political correctness has fed the trend of memory recovery. Possibly the most controversial writing on the subject of recovered memory is the 1988 book *The Courage to Heal*, by Ellen Bass and Laura Davis. Critics decry the book's sweeping generalizations, such as, "Many women don't have memories, and some never get memories. This doesn't mean they were not abused." Or, "If you think you were abused and your life shows symptoms, then you were." Most psychologists and psychiatrists reject the idea that any particular symptom or set of symptoms automatically indicates sexual abuse. They point out that neither author of *The Courage to Heal* is a licensed healer, and they are concerned that the introduction of repressed sexual abuse as the answer for a patient's problems may reduce the chance of identifying and treating another, real problem.

At the heart of the recovered-memory controversy—as well as the legal debate surrounding the admissibility of children's testimony in the courtroom—lies an acknowledgment that child abuse exists, along with a desire to find and punish those who commit it. Regardless of any changes in interviewing techniques or evidence admissibility, that basic desire won't go away any time soon.

Punishment or Treatment?

In Egyptian mythology, Anubis weighs the hearts of the dead against the weight of a feather of truth to determine whether or not they were virtuous in life. In the real world, of course, judging what is in a person's heart isn't nearly so simple. And when dealing with crime, that is essentially the final step. First the crime must be detected, evidence gathered, and a suspect charged. Next the suspect must be tried and convicted. Only then is judgment passed on the offender's heart—his or her moral culpability—and an appropriate punishment meted out.

As we have seen, the detection and prosecution of child abuse often present special difficulties such as the absence of witnesses, feelings of shame and embarrassment about discussing abuse outside the family, and questions about the validity of testimony. Deciding what to do with a convicted offender can be no less difficult. Obviously, much depends on the nature of the offense. When a child is physically abused or

A predatory stranger, every parent's nightmare. What is the best approach for stopping child sexual abusers? Expert opinions vary.

neglected by a parent, the first step may be to separate the child from the abusing adult—and when the abuse is severe and sustained, to terminate parental rights entirely. Severe physical abuse may also warrant a prison sentence.

Crimes involving sexual contact with children are usually treated differently. In the United States, such crimes have always been regarded as particularly serious, and there is much sentiment for harshly punishing offenders. But the issue is complicated by a basic question: Are adults who sexually abuse children merely criminal, or are they first and foremost mentally ill? From this question flow a host of others: Should sexual offenders receive long prison terms to punish or incapacitate them (prevent them from victimizing more children while they are behind bars)? Assuming that they'll be released eventually, will the prison term increase or decrease the chances they'll abuse again? Or should the emphasis be neither on punishment nor incapacitation but on treatment of the underlying mental illness that caused the offender's behavior—on trying to eliminate the offender's fantasies of having sex with children? Can a sexual offender ever be truly "cured"? And, if not, what level of risk should we accept when releasing a convicted sex offender back into society? These questions spur much disagreement.

Historically, punishment and treatment have alternated as the American judicial system's primary responses toward sex offenders. Early on, little tolerance existed for sex crimes. America's first recorded execution of a youth involved a 17th-century Massachusetts farm boy who engaged in sexual acts with a pet animal. Rape was punishable by death up until 1977. But the American judicial system has also periodically viewed sexual deviancy as a disease to be treated. Between 1937 and 1972, for example, 25 states and the District of Columbia passed laws allowing for the institutionalization rather than the imprisonment of sex offenders who were considered psychopaths. These statutes show the optimism associated with therapy during this period: with treatment, it was believed, sex offenders could be cured.

By 1990 most of the laws that allowed institutionalization had been repealed after medical and penal researchers cited the ineffectiveness of treatment. This disillusionment led to a return to punishment in the form of incarceration. Since then, however, skepticism about the value of imprisonment for sexual offenders has lingered. Given the low number of years served (typically as few as five for rape), officials are concerned about the rate of repeat offenses, or recidivism. Concern surrounding the release of convicted offenders back into society is now leading to mandatory therapy during a prison sentence. This therapy may range from group discussion to drugs aimed at reducing the offender's sex drive. Some within the legal community see mandatory therapy as a return to the assumptions behind the earlier institutionalization laws, and some place little faith in the ability of these programs to prevent recidivism when the offender is released. Others argue that the success of therapy depends on the nature of the crime and the motivation behind the offense.

Some therapists believe that treatment can indeed help sexual offenders overcome or control their problems, lessening the chances of a repeat offense. The National Institute for the Study, Prevention and Treatment of Sexual Trauma, headquartered in Baltimore, Maryland, has borrowed the techniques of alcoholism treatment. The institute makes clients confront their crimes while assuring them that they are not alone in their fantasies. Institute director Fred Berlin, who is also a psychiatrist at Johns Hopkins University, claims that "the child is to the pedophile [an adult who prefers sex with children] what the bottle is to the alcoholic." Berlin believes that, like alcoholism, sex

Right: Jesse Timmendequas, who had two previous convictions for child molestation, hears the guilty verdict in his trial for the kidnapping, rape, and murder of Megan Kanka. Opposite page: Megan Kanka's mother and brother are among those looking on as President Clinton signs "Megan's Law," May 17, 1996.

offending is a lifelong disease that can be managed but not cured. Others at the institute assert that the majority of sex offenders are not the murderers who make headlines, but instead are guilty of less invasive and less violent acts. This majority of offenders are people who like kids, and who in turn are liked by kids. The ability to befriend young victims, and the willingness to spend the time necessary to establish trust, is the reason a child molester is statistically more likely to be a friend or relative than a stranger. Rehabilitation, institute members believe, must be a top priority because it's not likely that a convicted sex offender will receive a life sentence, unless the victim is killed. And if the offender hasn't received treatment, upon release

from prison he will be likely to reoffend.

Today, many Americans are unwilling to put any faith in the rehabilitation of child sex offenders. For them the only issue is how to protect children from sexual "predators." A resurgence in this attitude can be traced to 1994, when a seven-year-old girl was sexually abused and murdered in New Jersey. Megan Kanka had been lured to the home of a neighbor, Jesse Timmendequas, by the promise of seeing his puppy. Instead Timmendequas raped and strangled her. Compounding the tragedy was the fact that Timmendequas had two previous convictions for child molesting.

A torrent of public outrage followed. Angry parents wondered how a convicted child abuser could be released into their neighborhood without their knowledge. They felt that released sex offenders created an invisible threat to the safety of their children. After more than 200,000 people signed a petition, New Jersey's legislature created a landmark package of interrelated sex-offender statutes that became known collectively as "Megan's Law." From those statutes three points, which legislators hoped would address the post-prison cycle of repeat offenses, emerged as the most critical and controversial:

1. Sex offenders released from prison must register with police where they live.
2. When a sex offender moves into a neighborhood, the community must be notified.
3. Sex offenders who have served their prison sentences but are deemed mentally ill and violent may be committed indefinitely to a mental institution.

Law enforcement authorities claim that the benefits of the first point—registering convicted sex offenders—are substantial. Not only does registration give police a jump in investigating sex crimes, it might also deter released sex offenders from reoffending because they know they can be traced. Civil libertarians, however, claim that registration constitutes an infringement upon the rights of individuals who have already "paid their debt to society" with a prison sentence. Advocates of registration counter that the legislature defines the "debt to society," and it may determine that the debt includes postprison monitoring.

The second controversial point is notification—distribution of the names or photographs of released sex offenders to the general population of the community where they live. Under Megan's Law, which became the model other states followed, three tiers of notification are used:

- First-tier notification—reaches law enforcement agencies and victims. Is intended to cover offenders considered at low risk of repeating their crimes.
- Second-tier notification—first-tier notification plus notification of community organizations (Boy Scouts, day care centers, and so on) that might be obvious targets for child molesters. Is intended to cover offenders who fail to comply with some aspects of their parole supervision, show little remorse for past crimes, abuse drugs or alcohol, or otherwise have a profile that places them at "some risk" of reoffending.
- Third-tier notification—first- and second-tier notification plus the possible notification of the entire

Community notification: A Portland, Maine, police officer hands out a leaflet informing a resident that a convicted child sex offender is living in her neighborhood. The woman's five-year-old son looks on.

community through the distribution of posters or fly-ers. Is intended for offenders who demonstrate repet-itive or compulsive behavior, show no remorse for previous offenses, were convicted of a violent act or used a weapon, or otherwise have a profile that places them at "high risk" of reoffending.

Once again the question as to why adults sexually abuse children becomes important. Without a defini-tive answer that can be uniformly applied to all sexual offenders, law enforcement agencies have difficulty determining which offenders are at risk of repeating their crimes. Dividing offenders into low-, moderate-, or high-risk groups is even more difficult, if not impos-sible. Because of this, critics of statutes such as Megan's Law argue that there is no way an offender can present a case for low risk and qualify for first-tier treatment. Plus, the final decision regarding level of notification rests with each prosecutor's office, and critics wonder whether prosecutors have the expertise to assess the risk an offender presents. They also believe that differ-ent prosecutors will inevitably use different criteria in making notification decisions. Because of the public and potentially harmful effect a second- or third-tier decision may have on a sex offender who is trying to live a normal life, critics say that the lack of uniform criteria for assigning the tier levels may violate consti-tutional standards of procedural due process. (Due process essentially dictates that everyone should be treated equally under the law.)

For the most part, however, through mid-1999 courts had upheld the registration and community notification provisions of state versions of Megan's Law. A June 1999 decision by the Pennsylvania Supreme Court was an exception. While the court let stand the provision in Pennsylvania's statute that required sex offenders classified as low risk to register their addresses with police after serving their prison sentences, it struck down the provision mandating that communities be notified when a high-risk "predator" moved into the area. The justices felt that classifying someone as a lifelong predator violated the presumption of innocence and was therefore "constitutionally repugnant." But the prosecutor in the original case was considering an appeal to the U.S. Supreme Court, which could decide once and for all whether Megan's Law statutes pass constitutional muster.

The third controversial point of Megan's Law—and it is by far the most controversial—allows the prisoner to be recategorized as mentally ill and held beyond the limit of the court-imposed sentence. As other states have followed New Jersey and enacted statutes allowing for the civil commitment of mentally ill and violent sex offenders, the controversy has heated up. Some critics charge that this provision makes the offender pay for the same crime twice. Others fear that, once again, assessing how dangerous an offender might be introduces a huge element of subjectivity into the process. And with continued confinement, the stakes are even higher than with community notification. Many see this as very dangerous ground.

"It's a long stretch from our system of due process and the standard of proof beyond a reasonable doubt to this prediction of future dangerousness," states attorney Kathleen Milner of the Minnesota Civil Liberties Union. "Conceivably after sex offenders they'll move on to other areas: 'Well, you're likely to shoplift again, so we're going to hold you.' "

To proponents, however, protecting children must be the paramount concern. It remains to be seen how frequently civil confinement following a prison term is used, under what circumstances such confinement may be constitutional, and what impact if any it has on lowering rates of abuse.

THE VICTIMS: WHERE ARE THEY NOW?

While the physical wounds of childhood abuse and neglect may heal, emotional and psychological scars can last a lifetime. Adult survivors of physical and sexual abuse may suffer such problems as low social competence, difficulty controlling behavior, depression, and appetite and sleep disorders. Survivors of severe neglect may display a range of self-destructive behaviors.

When experts refer to adult survivors, they acknowledge the lasting effects that child abuse may have on its victims. Many laypeople are apt to mistake a short-term solution—such as the removal of the Keystone kids from their Chicago apartment—for a long-term cure. The transition from child victim to adult survivor is much more complicated, and just as the circumstances surrounding abuse are different, the path to recovery varies.

The Keystone kids were started down the road to recovery by a determined judge assigned to their case. Many people had predicted that the children would eventually be returned to their mothers, as frequently happens in cases of abuse and neglect, but that did not occur. Several of the children have stayed together, and as they bond with their new families they have come to terms with the memories of their mothers and life at Keystone Avenue. It is at this point that media attention surrounding child abuse usually ends, as the

Children who have been sexually abused often grow up to be promiscuous adults and to engage in risky sexual behavior.

"success" or "failure" of the case is determined when the children are relocated and considered out of harm's way. That, however, is far from the real end of the story. The real end of the story is the way a child deals with, and hopefully overcomes, the long-term effects of abuse.

When children die as the result of abuse or neglect, they leave behind parents, grandparents, siblings, and neighbors who must contend with the tragedy. If the abuse was caused by a member of the family, other family members must resolve their own anger, guilt, and often embarrassment as intimate details of the family's life together are made public. It is for this reason that the names of child victims are often withheld from the media. Even if the abuser was not a family member, guilt and anger may still haunt the family: guilt that a child walked home alone from school or was injured while at day care; anger at a boyfriend, girlfriend, or baby-sitter who hurt the child. Siblings of the victim are especially vulnerable as they cope with their own fears (whether real or imagined) and struggle to understand the reaction of the adults in their family and what the crime means in their own life.

Victims who survive may face other psychological, behavioral, and physical problems in both the short and long term. Many of the short-term effects help health care professionals, educators, and social workers to detect child abuse. Unfortunately, the discovery and discontinuation of abuse, which may put an end to short-term effects, doesn't always prevent long-term ones. This is true for children who are neglected, physically abused, or sexually abused.

With over a half million documented cases of neglect occurring every year in the United States, there are a tremendous number of Keystone kids and Mitch Renfros who need help. The effect of neglect upon these children is of great concern. Many of the short-term problems associated with neglect are correctable if detected early. These problems include lags in physical development, ill health due to poor hygiene and nutrition, and fatigue. Unfortunately, ill effects may linger into adulthood in other forms. If the level of neglect was severe or sustained, mental and emotional development may permanently stagnate. Neglect during childhood may also contribute to later alcohol or drug abuse, sleep disorders, antisocial or destructive behavior, and a range of other behavior extremes. Consequently, the problems associated with neglect can be serious and are especially dangerous when caused by the consistent absence of elements considered crucial to a child's development, such as emotional support, good nutrition, and adequate medical care.

When children like Elisa Izquierdo and Brenda Miller are physically abused, the cuts, breaks, burns, and bruises are the short-term manifestations. While these physical injuries are dangerous and may cause permanent damage, they are only part of the problem. Another concern is that physical abuse has a physiological effect on the brain. Doctors at the Center on Neuroscience at The George Washington University in Washington, D.C., note that the brain, like other parts of the body, has an enormous capacity to repair itself during the most rapid state of a child's development, from birth to age three. This means that if abuse or neglect is detected early, a positive environment can repair the damage. Doctors emphasize a positive environment because the emotional and behavioral responses developed in childhood and used throughout an adult's life result from the way the brain deals with the trauma of physical abuse. The continued threat of physical abuse may undermine psychological healing even after the physical wounds have healed. Adult survivors of physical abuse may have problems such as the inability to control behavior, low social competence, and blunted psychological responses to the environment.

The frequency and predictability of abuse plays a role in determining the way the brain modulates behavior. With chronic, low-level abuse, a child develops adaptive defense mechanisms. On the other hand, doctors warn that unpredictable, intermittent abuse causes a child's stress responses to get bigger, a process called "kindling." The stress responses are the specific way a child responds to stress (for example, tears, violence, or withdrawal). Kindling may result in responses that do not match the abuse. When this happens the

Childhood abuse and neglect increase the risk of impulsive, violent, and criminal behavior later in life. But, experts stress, this outcome is by no means inevitable.

child may become violent or overly agitated when only slightly stressed or may not react at all when severely stressed or abused. This may even cause a seizure in the brain's limbic system, which affects emotional behavior. Dr. Frederick K. Goodwin of The George Washington University says, "Over time the brain will have the behavior on cue, even in the absence of stress." There-fore the behavioral problems resulting from childhood physical abuse may not be the mere repetition of learned responses—or an inability to break the cycle of violence—but could stem from damage done to the brain's function.

The short-term effects of sexual abuse include physical problems and age-inappropriate knowledge. Long-term effects are varied and are mostly the result of the emotional damage. The long-term behavioral effects of sexual abuse may include a violent personal-ity, social withdrawal, and self-mutilation. Psychologi-cal effects may include the confusion of emotional love with sexuality and a difficulty maintaining intimate relationships even if those relationships are not sexual. Other psychological effects range from depression and appetite and sleep disorders to multiple personality dis-order. While the development of multiple personality disorder is rare, researchers have found that almost all persons who suffer this condition were sexually abused. Finally, sexual abuse may lead to sexual dysfunction or lack of interest in sex as an adult, or to the sexual abuse of others and to promiscuity.

Doctors caution that there are large differences in how particular children react to abuse. If researchers could identify what makes some children resilient and others vulnerable, they could also identify the large group in between who are not affected in the long term. This would allow the development of individual pro-grams of therapy to better assist with emotional injuries. Experts are careful to caution against either understating or overstating the long-term problems associated with all forms of abuse. Certainly any child who was abused has been harmed, but amazingly, some children seem to suffer no long-term effects despite their horrifying ordeals. In the absence of stronger sci-entific evidence to explain why this might be, experts point to such factors as the child's easygoing temperament, high tolerance of frustration, and ability to develop emotional distance from an abusive parent. Other factors in the complicated formula are average or above-average intelligence and exposure to others outside the abusive atmosphere through extracurricular activities. These last two factors can play the largest role in eradicating long-term effects of neglect, as they provide the missing mental and emotional stimulation all children need.

The assumption that long-term effects of abuse will play an active role in the adult survivor's life can be as damaging as ignoring the possibility. Just as real-life instances of multiple personality disorder—popularized in movies like *Sybil*—are rare, an abused child does not have to follow the pattern and become an abuser. The more an abused child understands the cause or triggers that led to the abusive situation, the easier it will be for him or her to break the cycle of violence.

Unfortunately, many abused children do grow up thinking that they are unable to stop the cycle of abuse. Fears like this have grown out of the stereotypes society has created. Other harmful stereotypes have prevented boys from admitting they are being sexually abused by men out of fear of being labeled homosexual. In addition, society's treatment of the sexual relationship between a young male and an older woman as "the ultimate learning experience" creates conflicting emotions, making some boys reluctant to admit that they do not like the position they have been placed in by an adult woman.

Since the publication of "The Battered Child Syndrome," a multitude of help groups have formed to assist victims, families of victims, and even abusers. These groups have a variety of goals but typically focus on helping people understand the reason for the abuse, deal with the emotional response, and realize that others have faced the same problems and survived.

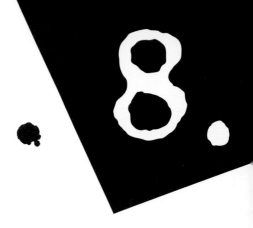

8.

THE FUTURE

As we have seen, attitudes toward child abuse and neglect have changed dramatically—not just since the Middle Ages but also in the past 100 years. Before, the treatment of children was not seen as a matter of government concern. Now, local and federal agencies exist to protect and support children. Before, parents' rights overrode the welfare of children, who didn't have any specific rights under the law until the late 1800s. Now, the courts try to balance parental rights with the welfare of children. Before, neglect and abuse were thought to affect only the poor, and class biases invariably accompanied the state's exercise of its *parens patriae* authority to take children from their parents. Now, we know that

New Hampshire police detective James McLaughlin (shown here in his office) has caught dozens of pedophiles who tried to lure their victims over the Internet. The online world has brought new concerns both for parents and for law enforcement.

the problems of abuse and neglect cross all socioeconomic boundaries, and the courts have ruled that
poverty alone cannot be used to justify breaking up a
family. In short, attention to the problem of child abuse
and neglect has never been greater, and the American
legal system has struggled to balance the rights and
interests of parents, children, and the state.

The role of children and the family continues to
evolve as a result of long-term trends in American society. The need for child care—which first arose during
World War II as large numbers of women went to work
in factories to support the war effort—has continued to
rise with the increase in the number of women in the
workforce and the number of children being raised in
single-parent households. During World War II, First
Lady Eleanor Roosevelt was instrumental in the pas-
sage of the first Federal Child Care Program to meet
this need. The 1968 enactment of the Federal Inter-
agency Day-Care Standards was an acknowledgment of
the continued need for child care and the first step
toward regulating day care facilities to create uniformly
safe environments.

But legislation also reflected America's growing
understanding that children faced dangers not simply
in day care facilities. The 1974 Child Abuse Prevention and Treatment Act laid down strict regulations for
the reporting of child abuse, and soon Dr. C. Henry
Kempe's 1962 warning about the prevalence of child
abuse was validated. In the 15 years following the Child
Abuse Prevention and Treatment Act, the number of
reported cases of child abuse increased fourfold as
physicians, teachers, and other officials responded to
the law requiring them to report suspected cases.

Unfortunately, acknowledging the seriousness of
the abuse problem and instituting reporting require-
ments haven't resulted in a solution. Throughout the
1990s, reported cases of child abuse remained frustrat-
ingly steady, hovering around 15 per 1,000 children,

according to child-advocacy groups.

Many parents and lawmakers say that popular culture adds to the difficulties they face when trying to protect children. The Internet specifically has introduced a new realm of potential problems. Through the Internet, children may be exposed to pornography without their parent's knowledge. An even greater danger is that children will "meet" individuals online who will make inappropriate advances, or worse, arrange a face-to-face meeting in order to sexually exploit them.

But laws designed to protect children on the Internet have to take into account broader issues such as the preservation of free-speech rights. The Supreme Court struck down the federal Communications Decency Act in the summer of 1997 because it unconstitutionally restricted freedom of speech. Advocates for children hope a New York law might be a model for keeping the online environment safe for kids while preserving everyone's right to free speech. The law makes it a crime to disseminate indecent material online to minors for the specific purpose of inducing them to engage in sexual acts. Accepted by both the American Civil Liberties Union (which regularly defends freedom of speech) and the National Center for Children and Families, the law has sent a clear signal that the Internet is not a tool for the abuse of children.

A 56-year-old man found this out the hard way. After they "met" on the Internet, he convinced a 13-year-old girl to meet him in person. When the girl turned out to be an adult undercover policewoman, the man became the first to be arrested under the "luring" law. For parents this only illustrates the potential dangers of the Internet. For law enforcement authorities it has meant expanding surveillance into new areas, hoping to deter criminals before children are injured.

In some ways the wheel has come full circle. At the turn of the century, children in the idealized middle-class family were separated from the world of their parents and

A safe, nurturing environment for all children is one of society's most important goals. While children in America today are better off overall than children have been at any point in history, the problems of child abuse and neglect persist.

provided a place apart from the problems of adulthood. Now children are central to the adult world even if their physical presence there is sometimes questioned.

The physical "place" of the child is evaporating. No longer do the majority of American children grow up with memories of long Saturday afternoons playing on the old corner lot or in the field behind the store. Children are now under constant surveillance by adults, for several reasons. Certainly many parents believe that, in the face of the nation's high crime rates, they must track their children's movements in order to protect them. But other parents are reacting to the changing standards of neglect. Letting the kids play around railroad tracks might have been acceptable 50 years ago, for example, but now it might be perceived as negligence on the part of the parent. Lastly, moral panic has a place in the caution, or overcaution, many parents exert in monitoring their children.

In general children are not interested in hearing about the dangers surrounding them. It is also difficult for parents to decide how much to tell their children about the possible threat of abuse. While many parents hate to burden even older children with "adult problems" or threats of abuse, this is especially true with young children. How old must children be before they can be told not to speak with strangers? How does a parent respond if a child asks why? Most parents generalize in their descriptions of imagined dangers in an effort to balance the protection of their children from an actual danger with protection from knowledge of dangers that may never emerge. This leaves a dilemma. How does a parent let a child know what flashing is, or that it is wrong? Or that certain words are inappropriate? To do this the parent has to be specific and must carefully consider the maturity level of the child and the circumstances of his or her individual environment. The same concerns affect the ability of a parent to respond to the needs of a child who has been abused either by another family member or friend or by a stranger. Medical professionals cite the immediate support that a child receives as a potentially major contributing factor in a smooth transition to recovery. However, the same health professionals caution that most parents are ill-prepared to handle the trauma of abuse, leaving them uncertain about how to best help their child.

Legislation is constantly adapting to the changing needs of both children and the judicial system. What is clear is that children have earned their place at the heart of statutes surrounding their defense. However, this does not mean that states are interested in casually terminating the rights of parents. Lawmakers across the country are forced to balance the rights of the family with the rights of the state when intervention may be necessary to protect endangered children. These decisions have been influenced by changing perceptions about the long-term effects of a stable environment versus a more transient (but perhaps physically safer) life in foster care. Decisions will also continue to be influenced by media attention to cases of particularly violent abuse, and eventually laws such as Megan's Law will probably be given the ultimate test—a hearing before the Supreme Court.

Within this common concern is the widespread clamor for strong (or longer) sentencing for those convicted of crimes against children. That clamor contrasts with the caution of many in the legal community against viewing prison sentences or therapy as the correct solution to the problem of child abuse and neglect. These experts advocate the use of funding to create a more service-oriented, preventive environment in which families at risk might live together—in the process, it is hoped, stabilizing the family and protecting the children. Experts fear that the emphasis on incarceration will continue to be only a stopgap measure that does not fully address the possibility of offenders repeating their crimes.

Despite differences in opinion about how quickly abused children should be removed to foster care from their biological families or how an abuser should be punished or reformed, it is clear that the welfare of children is center stage as the 21st century opens. Safety has become a priority of educators, law enforcement authorities, and social workers. As a result, children in America today are on the whole safer, healthier, better educated, and better protected by the law than they have ever been in the history of the world. And yet for a minority of kids, abuse and neglect remain a reality. How to change that situation is a problem that continues to perplex child welfare advocates even as it commands their attention.

Further Reading

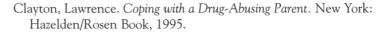

Clayton, Lawrence. *Coping with a Drug-Abusing Parent*. New York: Hazelden/Rosen Book, 1995.

Coman, Carolyn. *What Jamie Saw*. Arden, N.C.: Front Street, 1995.

Dolan, Edward F. *Child Abuse*. Danbury, Conn.: Franklin Watts, 1992.

Grant, Cynthia D. *White Horse*. New York: Atheneum Books for Young Readers, 1998.

Go Ask Alice Book of Answers. New York: Henry Holt and Co., 1998.

Hayden, Torey L. *Ghost Girl*. New York: Avon Books, 1991.

_____. *One Child*. New York: Avon Books, 1981.

Hodson, Phillip. *What Kids Really Want to Know About Sex*. London: Robson Books, 1993.

Johnson, Anthony Godby. *A Rock and a Hard Place: One Boy's Triumphant Story*. New York: Signet, 1994.

Johnson, Karen Cecilia. *Through the Tears*. Nashville, Tenn.: Broadman Press, 1993.

Magorian, Michelle. *Good Night, Mr. Tom*. New York: Harper Collins Publishers, 1981.

Moeri, Louise. *The Girl Who Lived on the Ferris Wheel*. New York: E. P. Dutton and Co., 1979.

Mufson, Susan, and Rachel Kranz. *Straight Talk About Child Abuse*. New York: Facts on File, 1991.

Peck, Richard. *Are You in the House Alone?* New York: Laurel-Leaf Books, 1976.

Pelzer, Dave. *A Child Called "It"*. Hollywood, Fla.: Health Communications, Inc., 1995.

_____. *The Lost Boy*. Hollywood, Fla.: Health Communications, Inc., 1997.

Silverman, Sue William. *Because I Remember Terror, Father I Remember You*. Athens: University of Georgia Press, 1996.

Voight, Cynthia. *When She Hollers*. New York: Scholastic, Inc., 1994.

Index

TRACEE DE HAHN is a freelance writer living in Lexington, Kentucky. Educated as an architect, she is currently pursuing a graduate degree in European History.

AUSTIN SARAT is William Nelson Cromwell Professor of Jurisprudence and Political Science at Amherst College, where he also chairs the Department of Law, Jurisprudence and Social Thought. Professor Sarat is the author or editor of 23 books and numerous scholarly articles. Among his books are *Law's Violence, Sitting in Judgment: Sentencing the White Collar Criminal,* and *Justice and Injustice in Law and Legal Theory.* He has received many academic awards and held several prestigious fellowships. He is President of the Law & Society Association and Chair of the Working Group on Law, Culture and the Humanities. In addition, he is a nationally recognized teacher and educator whose teaching has been featured in the *New York Times,* on the *Today* show, and on National Public Radio's *Fresh Air.*

Picture Credits